D0679071

intern

How to get the best internships and make them count

Andrew Scherer

Prentice Hall
is an imprint of

Harlow, England • London • New York • Boston • San Francisco • Toronto • Sydney • Singapore • Hong Kong
Tokyo • Seoul • Taipei • New Delhi • Cape Town • Madrid • Mexico City • Amsterdam • Munich • Paris • Milan

Pearson Education Limited
Edinburgh Gate
Harlow
Essex CM20 2JE
England

and Associated Companies throughout the world

Visit us on the World Wide Web at:
www.pearson.com/uk

First published 2011

ISBN 978–0–273–75665–1

British Library Cataloging-in-Publication Data
A catalogue record for this book is available from the British Library

Library of Congress Cataloging-in-Publication Data
Scherer, Andrew.
  Brilliant intern / Andrew Scherer
    p. cm.
  ISBN 978-0-273-75665-1 (pbk.)
  1. Internship programs--Great Britain. I. Title.
  LC1072.I58S34 2012
  378'.013--dc23
                                         2011030729

10 9 8 7 6 5 4 3 2 1
15 14 13 12 11

Typeset in 10/14pt Plantin Std by 3
Printed in Great Britain by Henry Ling Ltd., at the Dorset Press, Dorchester,
Dorset

Dedication

For my parents, Dion and Jane, and brother, Charles, for all their support over the years – with love.

Contents

About the author

Andrew Scherer (BA) read German at the University of Bristol and is marketing manager of Inspiring Interns (www.inspiringinterns.com), London's leading internship agency. In his job he has overseen almost 1,000 people complete internships, the majority of whom went on to earn full-time jobs at their companies. He was previously a journalist. Andrew completed several internships (some good, some bad) during university and immediately after, including a year-long placement in Germany. This is his first book.

Acknowledgements

Author

Many thanks to the entire Inspiring Interns team (particularly Benedict, Alex and Hannah) for their support, advice, suggestions and humour. This book would not have been possible without you. I am also indebted to Richard George of LinkedIn, Isla Grant of LawCareers.Net and Abu Bundu-Kamara of Pearson for agreeing to impart their plentiful knowledge in the Brilliant questions and answers. Finally, a great big thank you to Ben Rosen for coming up with the initial idea for the book and then trusting me with it!

Publisher

We are grateful to the following for permission to reproduce copyright material:

Text
Interview on pages 7-9 from Abu Bunda-Kamara, Pearson UK Diversity Manager; Interview on pages 17-18 from Isla Grant, LawCareers.net; Interview on pages 23-25 from Richard George, LinkedIn; Interview on pages 32-33 from Ben Rosen, CEO of Inspiring Interns

In some instances we have been unable to trace the owners of copyright material, and we would appreciate any information that would enable us to do so.

Introduction

Work experience in the UK traditionally has been characterised by brief periods of informal shadowing, often found through personal contacts. However, increasing numbers of school and university leavers are discovering that employers now demand more from potential employees than just academic qualifications. Thus, the concept of longer, more formalised periods of work experience – internships – has risen to prominence in recent years.

Brilliant Intern will help you plot a path through the still-developing internship landscape, pointing out common pitfalls, making helpful suggestions and generally being a useful guide to what is often the key to unlocking your future career.

Of course, the term 'internship' is still a very fluid idea and can mean many different things to different people. One company might use it to describe two weeks' of work experience full of photocopying and handing out mail. Another might consider it to be a year-long placement complete with a full salary, normal employee benefits and genuine responsibilities.

That said, most people are now making a distinction between shorter periods of 'work experience' and longer 'internships'. The former generally lasts less than a month and consists of little more than observing other employees doing their jobs and very occasionally doing small pieces of work. The latter usually takes place over a course of a number of months (often three) and includes structured learning through completing tasks under the supervision of permanent members of staff.

An internship is a big deal. It's not quite your first job, but it could lead to one. It won't tie you to one industry for the rest of your life, but could go a long way to plotting your career path. It won't cement your professional reputation, but could cultivate it. In short, a good internship has the potential to be a defining moment in your passage from student to worker.

At a time when a degree on its own is rarely enough to secure a job, an internship can help you develop a raft of qualities that will put you ahead of your peers in the hunt for a first job. With the cost of higher education rising significantly, well-structured internships are starting to offer a genuine (and significantly cheaper) alternative to Master's degrees and other aspects of higher education.

At the most basic level, spending several months in a professional environment confirms to a potential employer that you possess the fundamental skills required for work and will not come to them in need of intensive training. More significantly, it gives you a chance to show that you *can* transfer those oft-mentioned transferable skills from education to the workplace. Anyone can say they have 'strong analytical ability' and 'a good work ethic', but being able to point to three months where you used them in a work environment is of immeasurable value to a job application.

An internship is also a fantastic chance to get a real insight into a particular industry before committing to a job in it. It is all very well listening to careers talks about management consultancy or accountancy (for example) but, until you are actually exposed to the day-to-day routine involved in a job, can you really decide if it is something you want to do for the rest of your life?

Spending three months as an active member of a company also helps you develop a raft of new and relevant contacts, both within your host organisation and outside of it. If you make yourself useful during your placement, your name is likely to reach a number of different people within the firm who could have a bearing on your future. Equally, if you are in communication with other organisations, you will begin to develop a network within your industry.

All in all, an internship has the potential to be a crucial stage in your career. It is therefore wise to give as much thought to an internship as you might a potential job. There is little point sending half-hearted applications to positions you know little about and have even less interest in. Investing time in your internship, from application to completion, *will* reap rewards. It is an old cliché, but you really do get as much out of it as you put in.

PART 1

Finding an internship

There are thousands of internships out there and many different ways to locate them. Finding the right role is crucial to completing a successful internship and you should dedicate plenty of time on your search. This section will give you a broad number of techniques for finding sutiable positions and provide advice on how to impress potential employers.

CHAPTER 1

Selecting a sector

You have started thinking about your future career and have decided an internship would be a good way to kick-start your professional life. Fantastic – but what sort of area do you want to work in? Choosing a sector in which you want to gain experience should be given some thought. After all, this internship may end up influencing your career decisions for the next decade or more. So the big question that needs answering is: if an internship is (in part) a way to help me decide which industry I want to work in, how do I decide which industry I should do an internship in?

There are many similarities between how you select a sector you want to intern in and how you might look for a first job. Nevertheless, there are some key differences to bear in mind. This chapter will give you a good overview of the way to go about selecting an internship sector.

Your interests and skills

It is very easy to look at the well-advertised internships you heard about on campus and think 'they'll do'. But ask yourself whether you will really enjoy 12 weeks working as an accountant, whether that is the kind of experience you will find useful in the future, and whether you are just looking at it because a few of your friends mentioned it or you got a free pen from an accountancy firm at Freshers' Week. If working closely with businesses and numbers really does appeal to you, then brilliant – start applying for accountancy internships! If, having given it some real thought, you realise that accountancy may not actually suit your interests that much, then have a look at areas with which you feel a real affinity.

I don't wish to pick on accountants – as the old defence goes, some of my best friends are accountants – but it is a good example of an industry many students and graduates are attracted to, not because of a burning desire to be a financial bookkeeper, but simply because some big firms have a significant presence on campus.

It may seem a very obvious starting point, but why not begin your search for an internship by thinking about what your interests are? Massive football fan? You could start looking at a placement related to the sports sector. Bit of a fashionista? You might consider exploring the design industry. Of course, those are two obvious links to make, but try thinking about what you enjoy in life, and what positions may exist that relate to that.

Similarly, when identifying potential industries for your internship, try to match them with what you are good at. As I have already mentioned, many students and graduates are too quick to decide on a certain sector because of a bit of publicity they have seen from a major company, then get frustrated when they find their applications are not progressing as they might have hoped. Finding an industry where you can play to your strengths is, effectively, the first stage in a successful application. Giving serious thought now to what interests you and where your skills lie could save you realising, several years down the line, that you have made a serious mistake.

Research

There are lots of places that can give you a good overview of the different industries that graduates move into. Your university or school careers service will have plenty of literature and advice on many sectors out there. They will have seen plenty of people like you move from education to employment, and should have some good advice on what lurks beyond graduation. They may know if a particular industry has a history of providing internships, when they run, and which companies are best to approach. Careers services should also have an idea of what sectors people who were on the same course as you moved into – this might give you an idea of how graduates are applying the skills you are learning to the working world.

 **questions and answers**

Publishing internships

Abu Bundu-Kamara, Pearson's UK diversity manager, runs the Pearson Diversity Summer Internship Programme (PDSIP), aimed at ethnic minority graduates. It provides placements within one of Pearson's leading companies covering areas such as Publicity, Editorial, Sales, Communications, Business Administration and Finance. He talks to us about internships in publishing.

Q **What qualities do you look for in a publishing intern?**

A The first quality we look for in our candidates is an interest in our industries or the area the intern is applying for; if you're applying for an internship on the Journalism stream of the programme, we expect you to live and breathe journalism, or at least demonstrate a strong ability to write journalistically. As a company that thrives on creativity, content and communication we expect applicants to be good communicators – we look for people who are driven, express themselves clearly and succinctly and have a clear idea of what their career interests are.

Q Which is more important when hiring a Pearson Diversity Summer Intern – educational background or interest in the publishing industry?

A Educational background is, of course, very important to us when hiring a candidate, but it's not the be-all and end-all. We ask candidates for a 2:1 degree or equivalent qualification or experience; however, it's far more important that candidates have a well-rounded CV and a strong interest in the industries Pearson operates in and the area of the business they are applying to. For example, if you're applying for a marketing internship, we expect you to either have some work experience or extra-curricular experience in marketing, or strongly demonstrate how the skills and experience you have make you a suitable candidate for an internship in that area.

Q What will I learn from being a Pearson Diversity Summer Intern?

A Pearson interns learn a lot from this programme, not least how to work successfully within a global company. You have the opportunity to work with a variety of world-leading brands, including Penguin, *The Financial Times* and Pearson International. By doing this internship and undertaking a business-critical project, you get an opportunity from the first instance to learn the skills required for success in your chosen area. A key component of PDSIP is a Personal and Professional Development Programme, which focuses on helping you identify your professional strengths. The Development Programme is a two-day workshop that involves talks from high-profile speakers, workshops on key competency skills, as well as a CV and career-planning clinic. Throughout the internship, you're also coached on honing your networking and relationship-building skills, as well as having the opportunity through the company's Learning and Development Programme to attend a vast array of courses on skills you want to develop, from social media marketing to project management.

Q Do many of your interns go on to become permanent employees?

A Yes. Over the years, over 100 candidates have come onto the Pearson Diversity Summer Internship Programme. Though success on the internship programme is not a guarantee of a job, we place a great emphasis on retaining outstanding candidates on the programme at Pearson. Each year, many of these candidates are hired, as either temporary or permanent employees; our typical retention rate is between 50 and 70 per cent of all candidates on the programme. Even where we can't keep candidates, we maintain a good relationship with PDSIP alumni, and keep them abreast of relevant opportunities at Pearson.

Learn more: visit http://summerinternships.pearson.com

Once you have identified some potential sectors, try to find websites that carry industry-specific news (e.g. *PR Week* for public relations or *HR Magazine* for human resources). Have a good read of some of the stories there and see if they interest you at all. There are professional bodies for the majority of industries (e.g. the Chartered Institute of Professional Development for HR) which will have websites with plenty of information and advice about their own sector.

It is also worth scanning the business pages in the local and national press for ideas and inspiration. This will give you an idea of the kinds of industries that seem to be on the rise and, conversely, which industries appear to be in decline. Try targeting areas that seem to be growing: not only will this mean there is a greater chance companies will have available positions, it is also hugely important for your future job prospects. After all, do you really want to start a career in a sector that is shrinking and reducing the number of jobs available?

brilliant example

A great example of an industry enjoying major growth, despite the economic conditions, is mobile. With the advent of 3G networks and increasingly advanced smart phones, the scope of the mobile industry has broadened hugely in recent years. Increasing numbers of people are now   ▶

doing everyday tasks, like banking and shopping, on their handset and more and more companies are tapping into the potential of this exciting market.

With the sector enjoying such rapid growth, there are not only many internships and entry-level jobs opening up, but there is also fantastic scope for rapid career progression. Jobs in mobile can range from developing new apps to running advertising campaigns, so it is an industry that boasts opportunities for people with a diverse range of interests and qualifications.

Agencies

If you are able to muster only a vague idea of what it is you might like to do, or really have no idea what kinds of sectors are out there, it could well be worth signing up to an internship recruitment agency. Not only will they have a very good knowledge of the internship market, they should be able to offer tailored advice on what industry (or industries) they feel might suit your background and personality. Chapter 3 will look more closely at the role agencies can play in the internship hunt.

Keep an open mind

When it comes to choosing a sector, the major difference between interning and gaining full-time work is that your position is only temporary. There is, of course, a chance it might develop into a more permanent role, but there is no obligation for you to stay longer than you want. This control and flexibility make an internship the perfect opportunity to look at sectors you might otherwise have dismissed because you were not convinced they were quite right for you. If you already know that one industry is of interest, then try looking at related areas.

brilliant tip

Interested in writing and looking at journalism? PR, copywriting and online content creation all have similar requirements and will allow you to use similar skills.

If you have found an area you think you might find interesting but is yet to entirely convince you, then keep an open mind about it. While an internship can lead to your first job, it is also a time where you can afford to make mistakes and learn from them.

So, you've selected a sector (or sectors) in which you would like to do an internship. You are past the first important step – but you are now approaching the second. The following chapters will outline the different ways you can find the internships themselves, from applying online to less obvious methods.

brilliant recap

- When deciding on a sector, look beyond the obvious professions heavily promoted on campus.
- Identify your interests and skills, and find sectors that match these.
- Talk to careers advisors and use careers websites to build a better knowledge of different industries.
- Find industry-specific websites and news outlets that will give you an insight into their sector.
- Use the business pages in newspapers to establish new and growing sectors.
- If you have one industry in mind, consider other related areas.
- Be willing to take a risk!

CHAPTER 2

Advertised internships

N aturally, the first place you are likely to find internship opportunities is where companies decide to advertise them. As you might imagine, the vast majority of positions are advertised online, though we will take a quick look at potential offline sources too.

Internship-specific websites and job sites

Although internships are still a relatively new concept to the British job market, a number of websites already exist that are dedicated solely to advertising internships.

By far the most prominent of these is the government-run Graduate Talent Pool (GTP). The GTP is an online job board that allows employers to post opportunities and graduates to apply for them, all for free. The only stipulation for candidates is that they are a recent graduate (at the time of writing you needed to have finished higher education in 2008 or later). The roles advertised are based all around the UK, which is good news for those living away from the South East, which sometimes monopolises opportunities.

When the Graduate Talent Pool was launched in 2009 by the Department for Business, Innovation and Skills (BIS) it benefited from large amounts of advertising, which saw thousands of job-seekers and businesses sign up. Its popularity with both sides of the internship equation has endured and at any given time you can find 700+ positions advertised as well as thousands of registered candidates. This popularity has both positives and negatives when you are looking for an internship. The good news is that the Graduate Talent Pool is very likely to have some roles that will be of interest to you and in the location you want them. The bad news is that, with many other graduates logging on to GTP, the competition can be stiff.

> ### brilliant tip
>
> If you are still a student, there are websites dedicated to your requirements, too. Sites such as Freelancestudents.co.uk perform a similar role to GTP, but work only with those still in higher education.

Moving away from internship-specific sites, the more established job boards are now beginning to create dedicated internship sections on their websites. The likes of Reed, Totaljobs, Jobsite and Monster have all recently opened internship sections within their student and graduate pages. These sites initially may struggle to match the demand found on the GTP website but should build up a good range of opportunities. Like GTP, expect strong competition.

Industry sites

In the previous chapter we spoke briefly about using industry news sites and professional bodies to research different sectors. Most of these news sites carry their own job boards where lots of roles specific to that industry are advertised. Inevitably, the majority of these positions are senior jobs; however, you can also often find internships on offer. Similarly, many professional bodies may advertise vacancies. If they do not, they should point you in the direction of other places that carry relevant job advertisements. To find these sites simply google the relevant industry. You should find that the best websites will appear towards the top of the search results.

questions and answers

Law internships

Isla Grant, of LawCareers.Net, talks us through law internships.

Q What time of year do law internships take place and what is the application process?

A The large majority of firms run work placement schemes during the university summer vacation (although some also occur during the Christmas and Easter breaks). There is no centralised place to apply or to find out about which firm is offering what – rather, you have to check out the website of each firm you're interested in and see what their application requirements are. However, LawCareers.Net does have a list of deadlines: www.LawCareers.Net/Solicitors/WorkPlacementDeadlines.aspx

These days, most firms require you to complete an online application form for their scheme. You should consider this the first step of the recruitment process and, thus, give it your full attention, as if you were applying for a training contract. Firms attach a lot of weight to their vacation schemes, so consider it your first chance to shine.

Q Should I apply to as many firms as possible or target a small number?

A Without being too prescriptive about it, we think that somewhere between 10 and 20 is about right. As with training contract applications, you are better off making a handful of considered, well thought-out applications than taking a scatter-gun approach and applying to hundreds. So, identify those firms you're really interested in (looking at, for example, size, practice areas, location, ethos, training opportunities) and then spend time making your applications. Each application is likely ▶

to require several hours, so put in the time and hopefully it will reap rewards.

Q What sort of work can I expect to undertake during a law internship?

A The specifics will vary from firm to firm but, broadly speaking, you can expect to do some/all of the following: shadow a solicitor; research legal points; draft letters; attend client/internal meetings; go to court; and go to skills sessions. It's also essential to be proactive – don't sit and twiddle your thumbs if you feel like the work has dried up! Get out there, knock on doors and ask people if there's something you can help with. It's this kind of behaviour that will get you noticed.

Almost certainly, you will be invited to social activities as well – lunch with the partners, drinks with the trainees, nights out at comedy clubs, and so on. Take part in as much as you can, be enthusiastic and get involved – it will reflect well on you. But make sure you're remembered for the right reasons – i.e. being keen and helpful, not drunk and disorderly!

Q How important is doing an internship to receiving a training contract?

A Very important! More than ever, firms use their work placement schemes as a crucial part of their recruitment process – it is their first chance to see what you have to offer, how you cope in an office environment, and how you interact with your fellow students and members of the firm. So, while you're there, be conscious of the fact that you are being assessed – both formally and informally. Be yourself, but don't be so relaxed that you're viewed as not making an effort.

Equally, not getting onto a scheme doesn't mean that you won't get a training contract at the firm of your dreams. It just means that you have to work extra hard to impress at application and interview stage.

LawCareers.Net (www.LawCareers.Net) is one of the most sophisticated resources available to tomorrow's lawyers, today. Sections include news, the

Oracle, deadline timetable, diary of events, feature articles, blogs and much more.

There are several advantages to using such specific websites. Inevitably you will find positions far more relevant to your search than if you were using a more general job board. They should give you a good overview of what kinds of positions are out there, and how many are available. You may also find less competition, as the number of 'casual' applicants who make up part of your competition on general job boards will have decreased significantly. Casual applicants are those who may not have a serious interest in the role or sector but happened to see the position advertised on a general job board and thought they might apply.

University careers service

Another potential source of internship opportunities can be found through your university careers service. The number and range on offer will vary from university to university, but every careers service should have a selection of placements to offer you, and be able to point you in the direction of other potential outlets.

If you are still at university, do make the effort to pop into your careers office and talk with one of the advisors. They will be able to give you a good insight into what kind of vacancies they are receiving, and offer advice on what to do if they do not have suitable roles on offer. If you have graduated, or do not get the chance to visit the careers service in person, then their website should carry plenty of information on current vacancies on offer, as well as lots of advice around internships.

University careers services are often accused of pandering to the big boys in the corporate world and neglecting smaller companies, sometimes to the detriment of their students. While this accusation is not without grounds, more and more services have started working with local companies (often SMEs – small and medium enterprises) to create new internships for students and graduates. These can run alongside studies for those still studying, or can be full-time placements for graduates. The advantage of finding an internship through your careers service is that they are likely to have approved the company beforehand, so you can be confident they are a reputable firm. If, for whatever reason, you do encounter a problem during your internship you will also have a ready-made support platform to which you can turn. The disadvantage is many students go to university away from home so, if they are looking for an internship after graduation, or even in the summer months, their careers service will only be able to provide opportunities near the university itself.

Company websites

Although many companies advertise their internships as widely as they would a permanent job, plenty are less proactive when getting information about their placements out there. In practice, this generally means a firm's advertising for a new intern is limited to a small notice on their website. I would envisage this becoming increasingly rare as businesses wake up to the importance of internships but, for the moment, there are plenty of examples of employers adopting this laissez-faire approach to their placements.

Arguably, this is not desperately helpful for any potential interns but it does mean that, if you can locate any companies that have restricted their advertising this way, you will face limited competition for the position.

So how do you find these shy and retiring companies? A simple Google search will reap some rewards, but many good companies are likely to get lost in irrelevant results. Again, trade press and websites may well be your best source of information. Often they will carry lists of companies, usually divided by sub-sectors or specialities, the majority of which should be pertinent to your internship hunt. You could also try local business directories such as the *Yellow Pages*, which will list companies in your area by sector. Increasingly, these are also available online (e.g. www.yell.com).

It is then a case of poring through each firm's website. You should establish whether they (a) do something that matches your requirements and (b) project a company culture you feel you would fit with. You will then have to locate where they list their open vacancies (if at all). These can appear under many different sectors; some businesses may have a specific vacancies/employment tab on their home page, some may bury it in different sections such as 'About us' or 'Meet the team', others may just pop their openings into their company news.

Searching for an internship this way can be time-consuming and requires plenty of patience, but can also come with a big pay off – inevitably, if you do find good vacancies not listed elsewhere, you have placed yourself in a very small pool of potential candidates.

Social media

Social media has shaken up the employment market in recent years – for internships and beyond. You could probably fill a whole book on the changes to internship and job-hunting that have taken place, and continue to take place (I wouldn't be surprised if someone already has). This book will deal with social media – with all its benefits and pitfalls for interns – in greater detail in Part 2, but you cannot talk about finding an internship without mentioning it.

Essentially, you need to start thinking of Facebook, Twitter, blogs, etc. as a living, breathing job market, and start treating them as such. As an open job market, you will be able not only to locate job listings here, but also to be found as a potential candidate. The implications for this are far-reaching. Plenty of companies now use their Facebook page as a key part of their hiring process, and many also have specific Twitter channels dedicated solely to recruitment. This means that searching through social media websites often throws up relevant internship vacancies.

brilliant tip

There are even websites dedicated to helping you search social media for jobs. Twitjobsearch.com, for example, allows you to search for internships by sector and location. But don't forget to search websites such as Facebook and Twitter themselves!

The reverse side of this is you have to be very aware of who can access your personal profiles, and what these tell a potential recruiter. Allowing open access to your Facebook pictures, including that time you hilariously stole a traffic cone and put it on your head, won't necessarily recommend you to an employer for an internship. So, if your Facebook profile does contain some things you would rather keep among close friends, then check and double-check your privacy settings are at the right level. If you are on Twitter and do not restrict access to your tweets (the vast majority of people don't) then be careful that you do not start mouthing off or say something overly tasteless. You would be surprised how many people are watching. This is not to say you must be a lifeless drone online – employers do like to see that you are a real person with a personality – but just be aware what information you make available to the world. You are, in effect, presenting your personal brand.

Finally, there is a social media website designed for professional purposes: LinkedIn. Despite the fact it is a brilliant medium for finding work and networking, the majority of students and graduates do not use it. It is a terrible shame, as LinkedIn allows you to find so many useful contacts and job listings that are not available anywhere else. If you have not done so already, sign up now and start taking advantage of this brilliant resource.

 questions and answers

LinkedIn
Richard George, European PR manager of LinkedIn, gives some top advice on how to create a profile and make the most of it on the professional networking site.

Q What does LinkedIn offer potential interns, and how do I get started?

A For graduates and students looking ahead to their career post-university or looking for summer internships, LinkedIn provides direct access to the companies and decision makers who can help you in your first steps into the world of work.

Having a profile on LinkedIn is the first step. Your LinkedIn profile is often the first impression you make to potential employers; make sure you clearly describe what your aims are in terms of the careers you're interested in and what you've done to prepare yourself for them, whether that's the course you're studying or any extra-curricular activities that prove you're serious. Remember that LinkedIn is different from social networks; it's about making the right contacts to set you on the right course in your first job rather than sharing your Saturday night party photos.

Ensure your profile image is suitable. Is it clear and professional? Will people from that careers event recognise you? We're social animals and adding a professional-looking photo to your profile adds credibility. Plus everyone remembers a face.

Q How do students and graduates make connections on LinkedIn?

A Once you have a profile, you can start growing your network. A good profile greatly increases the chance of people accepting your invitation ▶

to connect. You may not have lots of connections in the business world yet, but you can look for your classmates, professors, tutors and any professionals you may have come into contact with during your time at university. Your network will soon begin to grow quickly as more people you know discover you. Your network is a reflection of your professional brand, so make sure to connect with people you know and trust.

Q How can I find people relevant to my internship search?

A You can use LinkedIn's Advanced search tool to find someone who might be in the career you're interested in, or even the hiring decision makers at the top five companies you want to work for. Quickly get from 100 million members to your shortlist by searching by name, keyword, title, company, location and industry.

You should also check out LinkedIn groups. There are hundreds of thousands of groups on LinkedIn where professionals from businesses of all sizes and sectors share insights and advice. If you're looking for quick and smart advice, check out some of the communities on LinkedIn. You'll find people in the companies you want to work for or doing the jobs you're interested in sharing their insights and even asking questions themselves.

Q What other ways can I get myself noticed?

A You can update your status on LinkedIn to let other people know what you have been doing – just make sure it will be valuable and interesting in a professional context. Have you just read an interesting business article or met someone who has shared some good career advice? Update your profile status regularly to make sure your network knows what you're up to. Seeing you share an interesting insight or story could be the trigger for someone getting in touch. It also keeps you front of mind.

You can also reach out to professors or tutors who you get on with and ask for a recommendation on your personal profile. If they accept, their personalised comments will appear on your profile for your other connections to see. Their own network will also see that they recommend you as someone with a bright future.

As with anything in the business world, you get out what you put in. LinkedIn is the same but the good news is, with a little giving, you can get a lot. Remember to encourage potential employers to come to you by sharing insights where you can, answering questions in a helpful way and generally demonstrating that you're keen and ready to learn. This is a great way to pitch your skills and potential.

To find out more about the latest openings for students and recent graduates, check out this recently launched LinkedIn Student Portal: www.linkedin.com/studentjobs.

Offline

Finally, there is still some value in exploring good old-fashioned adverts in print. Admittedly, many of these may well be duplicated online but there might be the odd one that appears only in a newspaper and you might kick yourself if you miss it.

National papers still carry daily job advertisement sections, often focusing on a different industry each day of the week (e.g. *The Guardian* has media vacancies on Mondays). You can find internships often listed alongside the permanent jobs, so it can be well worth having a look. Obviously it is expensive to buy a series of papers regularly, but you can get free access to them at your local library or even at your student union.

Local papers will also contain vacancies that you may not have seen elsewhere. So, next time one drops through your letter box, have a quick scan of the job pages before you throw it in the recycling.

 **recap**

- Check internship-specific websites, but be aware you may face plenty of competition.

- Also use the internship sections on more general job boards.

- Find industry news sites, most of which will carry job listings.

- Use your university careers service which may have internships exclusive to your university.

- Scout out individual company websites to uncover poorly advertised placements.

- Use social media to improve your 'personal brand' and as a new stream of potential companies.

- Don't ignore good old-fashioned newspapers!

CHAPTER 3

Internship agencies and recruitment services

With the growth in importance of internships in recent years, a number of companies have been created that seek to match candidates into placements with companies. There are some superb services out there, which can be a massive help when looking for an internship, and this chapter will take you through what using such companies usually involves.

Overview

Internship recruitment agencies work as middlemen in the application process, doing a lot of the legwork to make things as easy as possible for both you and the company. They will spend a lot of time seeking out businesses which are interested in hiring a student or graduate, ensuring they have a large selection of opportunities for candidates. On behalf of their clients they will advertise these vacancies as widely as possible, ensuring they get lots of exposure to potential interns. The agency will do some initial screening, which will vary for each firm, and then send their client a shortlist of potential interns from which the client will select people to interview.

Typically the agencies will charge their clients a fee for their services and are free for candidates. There are, however, some agencies that ask for money from potential interns. The majority of these specialise in helping British students find internships abroad, although some do have a domestic focus. It is prudent to be wary when paying money for services such as these, particularly as there are plenty of other options, which are free. If you do decide you are willing to pay a company for their help in finding you an internship, ensure you get some guarantee that they will refund your money if unsuccessful or the internship proves to be unsatisfactory.

University careers services sometimes have their own dedicated internship departments which perform a very similar service to private agencies. They may have fewer opportunities than dedicated recruitment services, but these may be exclusive to your university. Do be careful to distinguish between internship agencies and internship websites, like those mentioned in Chapter 2. As we shall see, the former will actively match you with vacancies and help you through the application process, while the latter is simply a place for employers to advertise internships and through which candidates can send applications.

This chapter will run through the normal process when applying to an internship recruitment agency.

Initial application

There are usually two ways to apply to an internship recruitment agency. If you know of a specific agency you can visit their website where all their vacancies will be listed. You can then browse through and see if they have any that are suitable. A good website should also allow you to apply for more than one position if several interest you. Alternatively, if you have a certain sector in mind but not a specific job, you should be able to send a speculative application, in which you can give a general outline of what sort of internship you are looking for.

Unfortunately, agencies often receive hundreds of applications a day so may not be able to reply to each individual candidate.

However, they should let you know the length of time it will take them to respond if they wish to continue your application, so you will know whether you have been successful or not.

Agency interview

If the agency decides to progress your application, you are likely to be invited into their office for a preliminary interview. The important thing to bear in mind is that this will be different from interviewing directly for an employer.

The agency may throw in some standard interview questions – 'Where do you see yourself in five years' time?' or 'Can you name a time when you have shown leadership skills?' – but these are to help the agency establish how comfortable you are interviewing, and get an overview of your background. The main purpose of the interview is for them to gain a strong understanding of your experience, your personality, your interests and your ambitions. They will not be trying to catch you out, they are simply getting to know you better. It is important that you are as open as possible with them as this will help them form a more accurate picture of you and your needs. Armed with this more in-depth information, they can go about finding you a suitable position.

If you have a very specific idea of what you want to do, then great – the agency should be able to help you move towards your goal. However, if you have only a vague idea of what sectors might interest you, or even what sectors are actually out there, then never fear. The agency should have experience of placing hundreds of graduates and students, and will be able to offer you some friendly guidance and assistance based on their experiences helping people like you.

If the agency has some roles they feel might suit you, then they may show you some different job descriptions to gauge your interest in different positions and tasks. Do not feel like you have to say yes to everything they put in front of you – a good agency will use your answers to build an even better picture of what kind of roles they should put you forward for.

Once you and the agency have mutually decided on some suitable roles, they will forward your profile to the relevant client or clients to look at. You should then hear shortly from the agency about whether the company would like to interview you.

In addition to meeting you, some agencies may offer other services, which will help you impress their clients, and allow the companies to gain a better understanding of you as a potential intern. For example, Inspiring Interns offers all the candidates who come into their offices the opportunity to film a short video CV. This short clip, usually 30–60 seconds long, gives you the chance to sell yourself by highlighting any areas you feel are particular strengths and generally showing you are more than a faceless CV and cover letter. They also offer the chance to undertake a psychological and personality test. This will measure your strengths and weaknesses, and give both you and the agency even more information to help identify relevant internships.

? brilliant questions and answers

Video CVs

Ben Rosen, CEO of Inspiring Interns, talks us through how to make a winning video CV.

Q Do employers really want to see video CVs?

A Because they are a relatively new phenomenon, video CVs are often dismissed by candidates as gimmicky or a bit of a waste of time. However, if they are used effectively, they can be an excellent tool in your hunt for an internship. Employers largely appreciate seeing someone talking to them rather than having to pore through yet another faceless paper application and it gives you a fantastic chance to convey your interest in a particular sector or role.

Q What should I include in my video CV?

A If you are filming a video CV at an agency, they should have all the basics in place but, if you are filming one at home, ensure you are in a quiet spot, will not be disturbed, and have a good light source. Keep the content short and to the point. Before you actually film, write down a quick list of what you want to say and memorise this. This will help you to avoid straying into irrelevant information. It should also help you minimise the number of 'ums' and 'aahs' in your video. However, do be careful not to make it sound too scripted: no employers want to hear a CV recited to them in a monotonous voice.

Q What should I leave out of my video CV?

A There is no need to list all of your experience and achievements: simply reading out your paper CV will do more harm to your application than good. Handpick your most relevant facets, much as you would for a cover letter, and explain why they make you a good fit for the internship.

Avoid bland, meaningless phrases that do not really tell the employer anything about you. Stating that you are 'motivated and enthusiastic, as well as a good team player' is boring and taken for granted. Differentiate yourself from the crowd.

For more advice and examples have a look at www.inspiringinterns.com/ video-guide/

Client interview

After your profile has been sent to a number of different companies, hopefully you will get a call from the recruitment agency within a week or so to let you know you have an interview. They will then liaise between you and the client to find a time that suits both parties.

The advantage of having an interview arranged through an agency is they will continue to provide you with support before, during and after it. They may well have some good inside knowledge on the company, which could be very useful to regurgitate when you meet them (particularly if you are facing other candidates who have not come from the same agency as you). Some firms also send candidates a text message on the day of their interview to remind them of the times and will call them afterwards to hear how it went.

After the interview, the agency will also be in touch with the client to see how it went from their side, and to get any feedback. They will then pass this (positive or negative) on to you so that, if you do not get this particular role, you can learn from the interview for future opportunities.

Placement

So, your interview was successful, you like the company and you have been offered the internship. Fantastic news! Part 2 will deal in much greater detail with what to do during your placement. However, it is worth noting a couple of points here that relate specifically to internships found through an agency.

Firstly, they will be in touch intermittently during the internship to check how everything is going and to hear what sorts of things you have been up to. Any good agency should take the time to check their candidate is doing OK and is happy with their placement.

Secondly, if you do encounter any problems during your placement, you should think of the internship agency as your safety net. Their work does not finish when they successfully find you a role, it is also their job to rectify any problems you may have. So, while your first port of call should always be your host company when trying to sort out any issues, do not be afraid to give your agency a ring or drop them an email if you need some help – they should be more than willing to lend a hand.

 brilliant recap

- Internship agencies will help you access suitable internship vacancies at a range of companies.

- They differ from internship websites by actively matching candidates with the roles rather than just advertising them.

- The process normally will be an initial online application, followed by a face-to-face meeting.

- They will offer support before, during and after interviews.

- Agencies will continue to offer help and assistance to you during the placement.

CHAPTER 4

Speculative applications and hidden internships

Sometimes, finding an internship is not quite as simple as looking for which companies are advertising for an intern and then sending an application, or turning up to an internship agency and letting them do most of the work. Unfortunately, many businesses might be interested in hiring an intern but the task remains towards the bottom of their priorities and positions go unadvertised. Other companies may not have even thought about taking on an intern, or do not fully understand what is still a developing concept in the United Kingdom, so have put off giving it serious consideration.

Unlike trying to fill a full-time role, where there is an obvious and immediate demand for an additional member of staff, offering an internship is often not a pressing issue for companies. This means there is plenty of scope for potential interns to smoke out opportunities that do exist but very few people are aware of.

The huge advantage in taking this approach is that your competition will be very limited, giving you an excellent chance of landing a position if you are the kind of person the company is looking for. They are certainly more likely to be flexible on their requirements if far fewer people are applying for the internship. You also have immediate proof of your desire and perseverance to work in the industry and for that firm: you were able to find out that they were interested in hiring an intern despite the fact they were not advertising!

The big drawback to this approach is that it is very time-consuming, requires plenty of resolve, and can be down-heartening: be prepared to receive plenty of rejections and even more empty silences in response to your applications. Don't let this put you off attempting to find those hidden internships – it can be a great route to go down – but let it serve as a warning that this is no walk in the park.

So, got a suitably resolute face and your thinking cap on? Well, let's have a look at how to go about finding those elusive placements.

Target individual companies

If you have undertaken thorough research into your sector and the various companies that operate therein, almost certainly you will have come across a few businesses that look like they would be a good match for your internship but currently are not hiring interns.

Similarly, if you have been keeping an eye on relevant industry news, you may well have spotted a company that is growing quickly or has recently received some investment. These organisations are prime targets for potential interns: there is a very good chance they will be looking for additional people to join the team, particularly bright and enthusiastic students and graduates. Having identified potential companies, you need to go about compiling an application.

Chapter 6 will examine in far greater detail how to put together a winning internship cover letter and CV, but it is worth highlighting some key pointers when applying speculatively. Firstly, make it abundantly clear why you have alighted upon a company as a potential host of your internship. Secondly, tailor your CV so that it fits with the company's own background and specialities. Applying to a marketing firm with a strong social media department? Be sure to highlight your digital know-how. Thirdly, be polite, but not grovelling. Thank the person reading your cover letter for their time, but refrain from commenting on their generosity, their selflessness or their humanity for having a quick glance at your CV.

One of the most important aspects of sending a speculative application is ensuring it reaches the right pair of eyes. There is little point spending hours crafting, honing and personalising your cover letter only to spend 30 seconds on a company website until you find their generic 'info@' email address and sending it to an anonymous inbox. If getting an internship at a firm really means so much to you, is it really worth relying on the person who only checks the info email once a week taking the time to pick your message out from hundreds of other pieces of correspondence and forwarding it to the relevant party?

brilliant tip

Some businesses will go as far as automatically rejecting any applications to their generic email, as they feel it shows a lack of interest and commitment from the candidate. So make the effort to find the right person to contact!

Don't be the person whose CV gets dragged straight into the trash can. Spend some time on the company website and see if you can establish who might be the right person to email. If you are unsure, make an intelligent guess (hint: an intelligent guess is not sending your application for a marketing internship to the IT department, nor is it blanket emailing everyone in the company). Offer your apologies in the body of the email if you have guessed wrongly ('I am sorry if you are not the right person to contact. If you could forward my message to the relevant department, I would be hugely grateful').

If you have the right person but no email address, try using the many social media sites to find it. Many professionals list their email address on LinkedIn or even Twitter, so do not be afraid to search for it. Why not try googling the person in question as well – this can unearth useful contact details.

Many candidates often overlook the good old-fashioned phone as a way of finding out important information. There are plenty of companies that will happily let you know the best email address to which to send an internship application if you take the time to give them a call. It can be worth doing this before starting to write your cover letter too, as they may also tell you whether there is any chance they will take you on.

Personal contacts

Whether you realise it or not, throughout your life you have already built up a network of contacts who may be useful when searching for an internship. Family, friends, friends' parents, teachers, old bosses and colleagues – any of these could (unknowingly) hold the key to finding you a placement. You need to let these people know that you are on the internship hunt, and what sort of thing you are looking for. How you go about this really depends on your relationship with the person in question.

Clearly, for close friends and family, you need only mention to them that you are looking, and ask if they know anyone who could help out in any way. If they do have a contact that might be useful, ask for their details, but also get your friend to check it is OK for you to get in touch. They will then be expecting a message from you and are more likely to offer a response, even if they cannot help out this time.

Quite often, you may have to delve deeper into your network than your immediate family and closest friends to discover useful contacts. Previously, this might have been a fairly laborious task. However, the advent of social media has made it a far easier undertaking. How many friends have you got on Facebook, for example? Do you use Twitter? Then tweet what you are after. Hashtag key words so they are easily searchable. Again, you never know who from your online network is watching.

brilliant example

Update your Facebook status, explaining any help in your internship search would be much appreciated and, suddenly, everyone knows what you are after and can help out if they are able to. Why not change the strange little box under your profile picture to a quick description of what you are looking for – you never know who will see it.

As we've already seen, LinkedIn is a hugely valuable tool that is criminally underused by graduates. So, if you haven't already signed up, do so now and start adding as many people you know as you can find. LinkedIn will then display how many people you can reach through your extended networks, and give you a far better chance of locating relevant parties.

The other, more formal, route to go down for finding related personal contacts is using your pre-existing professional network. Given you are probably still in, or just out of, education you may think that this is practically non-existent, but you would be surprised how many potential contacts you have. Former teachers are often pleased to hear from their old pupils and usually are more than happy to help them out, so try getting back in touch with them. They or the school itself may have some handy connections, perhaps through their alumni association, which are worth exploiting. You may find employers, rightly or wrongly, are more open to candidates who went to the same school as they did. At the very least, it offers the chance for some light-hearted small talk at an interview!

Similar to using school contacts, exploring your university network can also be rewarding. Lecturers and tutors may know of former students who are relevant to your internship search, and many careers departments carry lists of graduates who have said explicitly that they are happy to be contacted by other students and graduates for advice and sometimes even offer placement opportunities. If your university does have such a scheme, it is likely their alumni network will hold at least one very useful contact for you.

Finally, think back to any paid work you have done and who you worked with or for. It may not seem at all pertinent to what you are looking for now, but your old boss may have connections with different industries, and your old colleagues may have moved on to pastures new – pastures in which you might want to join them.

Essentially, if you explore your personal network fully, including the less obvious paths, there is a good chance you will find some relevant people to talk to about your internship hunt.

Get imaginative

Sometimes, if you want to flush out those hidden and unadvertised opportunities, you have to start thinking outside the box. This is particularly true of candidates looking to find a placement in highly competitive creative industries, but does also apply to those looking for more traditional business-centred roles.

This might be something as simple as cutting your CV down to a minimalist one page with a stand-out design, or you may look to do something a bit grander. The main point of getting inventive when trying to find an internship is to stand out from the large crowd that makes up your competition.

brilliant tip

I heard a great story recently of a graphic design graduate who had sent her portfolio, which was of a very high standard, to scores and scores of companies, as she sought to do an internship. She either received swift rejections or, more often than not, no response whatsoever. So, using her creative nous, she baked a batch of gingerbread men and decorated them with key details from her CV. She then packaged them in professional-looking cellophane bags, tied them with some nice ribbon, and hand-delivered them to six different companies. She got six interviews.

There was also a recent story that made the national press of a graduate, looking to gain any kind of business experience, walking up and down the Strand and Fleet Street with a sandwich board advertising himself. It simply had his name, his university, his degree and a contact number on. By showing such initiative, he ended the day with a series of internship offers.

It is easy to dismiss such stunts as gimmicky but, clearly, many employers like to see candidates demonstrate such ingenuity and dynamism. It will not work for everyone but, for some, taking a slightly more unorthodox approach to internship hunting could reap major rewards.

 recap

- There are hidden internships out there waiting to be discovered.

- It may well take some hard work to find them.

- Find companies you like the look of and target them.

- Explore your entire personal network – you will be surprised at what useful links it throws up.

- Get creative and stand out from the crowd. Make sure someone takes notice of your application.

CHAPTER 5

How to avoid bad internships

Sadly, not all internships turn out to be particularly useful or beneficial for the intern. There are generally two ways in which a placement can turn out to be a 'bad' internship.

The first is deliberate malpractice on the part of the employer. You may well have read horror stories in newspapers of unpaid 'interns' being forced to perform basic cleaning duties or run unpleasant errands in the name of gaining relevant experience. These are, of course, not internships at all, just unscrupulous companies using the mantle to justify exploiting young workers. This stems partially from the fact that internships are still a new and evolving concept in the UK and are yet to find a firm place in employment law, leaving a bit more room for some people to exploit the system. However, please do not let the existence of a few questionable firms put you off. A proper internship can be a hugely beneficial experience for both intern and host company. I simply would urge you to read this chapter to ensure you avoid becoming the one being taken advantage of.

The second classification is less of a 'bad' internship, and more of a badly matched internship. Away from the extreme end of poor experiences, a bad internship for one person might be a good internship for another. A lot of what combines to create the internship you want will be subjective. So there is an onus on you to find out as much as you can about the position before you accept it and then decide whether it matches your requirements.

Don't forget, it is not just about a company picking you – it is also about you picking a company.

This chapter will help you both avoid the exploitative internships, and ensure you are a good fit for a placement before you start it.

Source of internship

A key thing to bear in mind when avoiding a bad internship is the source where you originally found it. If it is from a reputable source, you should have fewer concerns about its quality; if it is from a less well-monitored source, you should be a little bit more careful. That is not to say there are hundreds of low-quality internships waiting out there, but that you should exercise a sensible level of wariness if the internship has come from somewhere that has not already verified its calibre. In much the same way you wouldn't buy concert tickets from someone on eBay without first checking they were a reputable seller, so you shouldn't dive headlong into an internship if it hasn't been properly scrutinised.

 **brilliant** timesaver

If you have found an internship through an agency or university, then they should be able to attest to its quality, certainly if they are a reputable firm. Ideally, they will have met already with the company to assess the office, the culture, and find out exactly what it is the business wants from an intern. They can then pass this information to you to help you decide if the placement is a good fit. You should still ask relevant questions of both the agency and the company itself, if you end up meeting them, but the fact that checks have already been carried out should give you some peace of mind. The other advantage of using an agency is their continued support throughout the placement, so, if things do not go as planned, you know you have someone on hand to help deal with things.

If you find your internship through a job board, I would be a little more cautious. You may take some comfort in the fact the Graduate Talent Pool is run by the government, but do bear in mind that they do not necessarily monitor all the content on the site. They may well block adverts that explicitly contravene posting rules, but that does not mean that every advert gets thoroughly researched before it is posted. Indeed, there has been some criticism that the GTP is too open and should clamp down on the more vague listings that appear on it. So, if your opportunity has been found on GTP, be sure to conduct thorough research into the company and the internship. This goes for other major job boards too, such as Reed and Totaljobs.

Let me reiterate that the vast majority of listings you come across will be legitimate internship opportunities, and you should not presume a company is hiding something. However, because there are a few rogue listings out there, it is important to use your common sense and do a bit of background research to ensure you do not get caught out.

Goals of internship

One excellent way of making sure both you and your potential host company are fully briefed on what to expect from the internship is to have a clearly defined list of goals for the placement.

A good internship advertisement will set out the goals and learning objectives involved in the placement explicitly. If you find a more vague listing, with fewer details on what you will be doing and what you can expect to gain from the position, do not presume that it is a bad internship. Do, however, spend time finding out more about what the placement will involve and what you can expect to learn.

Some internships will centre around one specific project. If this is the case, the employer should have little difficulty in telling you exactly what sort of work you will be assisting with, what the objectives of the internship are from their point of view, and what you will be learning over the course of the project.

If the internship is of a more general nature, then the employer should be able to outline the sorts of tasks you will join in with, roughly what to expect on a day-to-day basis, and again give you a basic idea of the kinds of skills this will help you develop. Of course, if these do not match with what you are looking for, do not be afraid to politely withdraw your application.

It may be that the employer has not given much thought to exactly what sort of work the intern will be involved in. Your questions could prompt them to spend a bit more time coming up with a solid plan for the intern. Also, be aware that some internships are intended to have a degree of flexibility to allow them to naturally progress into the areas that most interest the intern. If, however, the employer really cannot (or will not) give you a good idea of what you will be doing and learning, then think carefully before agreeing to join.

I am not in the business of warning you off internships and there will be companies that offer beneficial experiences to interns without being able to give much information beforehand (if they haven't run a programme before, for example). Nevertheless, the more you know about an internship, the more confident you can be that it won't be a bad match for you.

Mentor

Before starting an internship it is important to establish whether you will have a specific mentor at your host company and, if so, who it will be. This will not necessarily be the person who has direct responsibility for you. Often it is beneficial to have someone who is not directly involved with your work who you can talk to and who can offer you advice and guidance.

If you are working in a smaller company, it is unlikely that they will be able to offer a separate mentor. This is absolutely fine, but make sure you have established who you can talk to in the company about your progress and what level of support to expect from them. We will talk more about mentors in Part 2 of the book.

Company culture

When trying to avoid bad internships, be careful not to overlook the company culture where you will be working. Of course, making sure you will be stimulated, learning relevant skills and doing things that interest you are key to finding a good internship. However, the culture of the workplace you find yourself in can be surprisingly influential on how much you get out of the placement. It is much harder to learn and to form relationships (which is a key part of an internship) if you are in an environment that does not suit your personality. So keep a particular eye out online for any clues to a company's culture. Their website can tell you only so much: looking at employees on LinkedIn, finding if they have any videos on YouTube, even checking the tone of their tweets, can provide interesting insights into whether you will fit in with their team.

However, you can garner only so much information on company culture from the internet or hearsay. It is therefore very important to be aware of the office surroundings if you are asked to an interview. An office that is a hive of activity blasting out loud music could be detrimental to your development, if you consider yourself a bit of a wallflower. Similarly, if you are outgoing and lively, then working in a silent, highly focused office may actually stifle your progress.

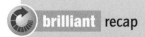 recap

- They are rare, but be aware of companies that may try to take advantage of their interns.

- Make sure the internship is a good match for your requirements.

- Check the host firm has a clear idea of the goals of the internship, both for you and for them.

- Ask whether you will have a specific mentor and whether they will be your line manager or (in larger companies) someone from a different department.

- Investigate the company culture to establish whether you will fit in well.

- Do not be afraid to ask these questions; an employer will respect the fact you are taking the internship opportunity so seriously.

CHAPTER 6

CVs and cover letters

Once you have found an internship (or more likely several internships) for which you would like to apply, you need to prepare your cover letter and CV. Do not fall into the trap of thinking that because this is 'just' an internship that you can get away with a five-line cover letter and a semi-updated CV. Employers, particularly those who are taking their internship programme seriously, will expect to see high-quality applications that have been given as much care and attention as a job application.

There is lots of advice to be found elsewhere on how to put together a winning CV and cover letter (*Brilliant CV* and *Brilliant Cover Letter* for a start), so this section will touch only on the basics. It will focus instead on the specific things you can do to make sure your CV and cover letter are optimised for an internship application.

The biggest and most frequent mistake made with cover letters is to send generic versions for every application you make. For an employer flicking through scores of different candidates, there is nothing like a general cover letter to fast-track an application to the reject pile. Make sure yours stands out by making it very specific to the internship and company in question. However, the personalisation quest does not end there. Your CV should also be finely honed to ensure it closely matches what the employer is looking for. This chapter will give you some guidance on tailoring your CV and cover letter for internship opportunities, with particular focus on what you should and should not include to help you stand out from the crowd and get noticed.

Cover letter

Writing a cover letter is your chance to convey your interest in, and suitability for, the internship position that has caught your attention. It is an opportunity to sell yourself and make the person reading your application sit up and take notice of your CV.

As with a cover letter for a normal job application, it is important to demonstrate a good understanding of what the role will entail, and match that with your background, skills and interests. In reality this should be little more than a quick comprehension exercise: if you carefully read the advert you have seen you should have a solid idea of what the internship involves. Show this by stating, with examples, how your own CV corresponds to the requirements of the position. As it is an internship you should not be afraid of saying that you wish to develop some of the skills required for the role, but ensure that you can point to something on your CV that at least demonstrates a prior interest in the area. For example, it is fine to apply to a journalism internship with little or no professional experience – this is what the internship is for – but you should be able to illustrate an interest in writing through extra-curricular activities such as helping on your student paper or running your own blog.

Similar to demonstrating your understanding of the internship in question, your cover letter needs to provide evidence that you have researched the company properly and offer an explanation as to why you feel you would fit into it well. Much as you have done with the specific role, you should read the advert closely for information on the business, and also visit their website to get a really good feel for what they are about.

brilliant tip

The best candidates will go beyond regurgitating website copy on their cover letter. They will dig a bit deeper and find more information on Google, Facebook, Twitter, in fact any number of sources, to build a rounded and impressive overview of the company.

If you are writing a cover letter for a speculative application, you will naturally have no advert to feed off. This means it is even more important to show what you have to offer the company in question and you should focus more on linking this to what you know about the firm's work and its culture.

As this cover letter is specifically for an internship, it is also worth mentioning what you personally want to get out of the experience. What skills are you keen to develop? What part of the industry do you hope to improve your understanding of? Which part of the internship do you think you will enjoy most? This is another great way to show that, not only have you given the position plenty of thought, but you are prepared to offer commitment and real effort to the role.

You may also wish to consider making reference to your availability for a permanent position, should you be accepted and the internship goes well. I would not advise doing this on every application, and certainly not for speculative ones, but, if the advert does make reference to the potential for permanent employment after the placement, it is a point worth raising. This will, once again, show the person hiring that you are prepared to really commit yourself to the internship (and beyond) and, on a practical level, may be useful to the employer for their planning.

CV

Writing a CV for an internship application does differ from writing one for a full-time job. The main variant is the fact that your professional experience inevitably will be limited and employers will be looking more closely at things like education and extra-curricular activities. Do not be concerned by a lack of work experience and, certainly, do not try to exaggerate or overemphasise it. Employers are looking for potential in interns, so use your CV to convey your enthusiasm and interest in the sector and role.

With lots of competition for internships and limited experience to differentiate yourself from other candidates, it is key that you make your CV as presentable and as easy to read as possible. It should *never* be longer than two sides and, ideally, you should try to fit everything onto one page. A 'one-pager' not only looks slicker, it is easier for any potential employers to glance through and pick out information. If you are concerned that you will not be able to fit everything onto one side of A4 then remember: you are not trying to give a life history, just a quick overview of relevant things you have done. You can highlight the most important points in a little more depth in your cover letter. Also, ensure the page does not look too crowded, and that you have used the same plain font throughout, and formatted everything properly (e.g. no random indentations or floating paragraphs). Essentially, do what you can to make your CV appear easily accessible and readable. It may seem a little superficial, but, if the person reading your CV has already waded through 50 others, you need to make it as easy as possible for him or her to like yours.

brilliant dos and don'ts

CV presentation

Do

- ✔ Consider limiting your CV to just one page
- ✔ Use a plain font
- ✔ Put education above employment
- ✔ Check all bullet points and paragraphs are properly aligned

Don't

- ✗ Ever go over two sides of A4
- ✗ Change your font at any point, apart from the heading

At the top of your CV should be your name (in larger font), followed by your basic details, including phone number, email address and home address. Be aware that it can have a negative impact on your application if the address you put is nowhere near the internship for which you are applying. For example, if you are studying in Newcastle and are applying for a placement near your family home in London, put down your parents' address and not your term-time one. If you are planning on staying with friends or family during a potential internship, make it clear in your cover letter that you will be staying within commutable distance. If you have two email addresses – for example a personal one and a university one – use the account you check most often.

After giving your basic details, a personal statement is an excellent way to start your CV. It gives you a chance to explain, in a succinct and targeted manner, why your background makes you right for the role. If you have little relevant work experience, this can be crucial for a potential intern to help the employer link the contents of the CV with the role.

The key to a good personal statement is to be specific. Anyone can write bland general statements professing themselves to be a 'natural leader' or 'enthusiastic and dedicated'. These basic facets are taken as a given by employers – very few potential interns will admit to being bad with people and apathetic towards work. Rather, an internship personal statement should say exactly what has attracted you to the role and sector. You should then briefly outline what you have learned that is relevant to the position and perhaps the things you want to learn. If you do have any relevant experience, you can mention it here too. A good, relevant personal statement immediately elevates your CV above anyone who has not bothered to tailor theirs and makes your application far more competitive.

 **brilliant** example

CV personal statement

Bad

I am an enthusiastic and motivated Geography student in my final year at Loughborough University. I am looking for an internship in HR as I am good with people and feel working in this sector would suit my people skills. Having worked in the food department at Marks & Spencer last summer, I feel I gained a great understanding of how HR works, having dealt with the HR team there several times.

Good

I am looking for a Human Resources internship to build on the skills and knowledge gained from my Geography degree at Loughborough University. Having chosen to specialise in the psychological aspects of Human Geography, I have a good understanding of people's motivations and interactions, a facet which I believe transfers well to HR. I am keen to develop these skills within a professional context. In addition to my summer work at Marks & Spencer, I spent several days observing their head office

HR team. Seeing the work they did, from screening candidates to resolving internal staff issues, added to my desire to build a career in this fascinating sector.

The first thing after your personal statement should always be your education. Lots of candidates think they can give the impression they have a huge amount of work experience by listing all their previous jobs early in their CV, then adding their education at the end. Not only do employers see right through this, it suggests you are a bit blasé about your degree or A levels, or even that you are trying to disguise them. Always put your education first on an internship CV: undoubtedly you will have been learning for longer than you have been working, and it will demonstrate your general competence far better than a couple of part-time summer jobs. If you have completed any modules that are relevant to the role, then list those too (for example, an accountancy unit within your business degree). Do not, however, list every topic you have studied – they will be largely irrelevant to the position you want.

brilliant impact

When choosing what to include in your CV, always ask yourself the following questions.

- Does this show an interest in the role?
- Does this show a passion for the sector?
- Does this show a skill the employer will value?

If it does none of these things, then there is probably little point putting it on your CV.

After you have outlined your education you can then intro-duce your working history. Some people will prefer to do this chronologically, some people prefer to group experience by skills. If the most relevant parts of your employment background happened relatively recently, then a chronological list will be fine. However, if they are further back, then it is a good idea not to bury them towards the bottom of your CV. You do not need to list every single duty or task you were charged with in each job, but pick out the most relevant ones and also highlight a few that show general competence and responsibility. Do not try to list every single piece of work you have ever done to beef up this section – going too far back or being too broad in your inclusions can serve to dilute the more meaningful work you have done.

Do not be concerned if your employment history is relatively short – an internship is designed to help you develop this section. More important is the ability to convey your enthusiasm for a certain sector or role. Listing your achievements, interests and activities is a great way to do this. This should not be an exhaustive list of all the things you enjoy doing in your spare time. However, do mention anything that demonstrates a prior interest in the area of the internship. By way of example, if you are applying for a graphic design placement, you might want to talk about how you designed a poster for a university event, or helped produce a student magazine cover. You can also include major achievements in your life, such as undertaking a gap year or completing voluntary work – as ever, highlight the most relevant parts: responsibilities, independence and initiative.

 brilliant recap

- Always tailor your CV and cover letter to each different application.
- In your cover letter show that you understand the role and the company, then demonstrate how they match your profile.

- Do not be afraid to say what skills you want to develop – this is the point of an internship.

- If the employer mentions the potential for permanent employment after the internship, state if you are interested and give availability.

- Target your CV personal statement, avoiding clichés and meaningless buzzwords.

- Always put education above employment history.

- Arrange your CV so the most relevant points for the position are the most accessible.

CHAPTER 7

Interviews

Much like your internship CV, you can expect your internship interview to differ from one for a full job. The guiding principle for the employer is the same as it was when they first looked at your application – they are looking to find your potential and enthusiasm for the sector rather than testing your experience of working within it. With that in mind, this chapter will guide you through what to expect from your internship interview, offer some tips on general preparations, and advise what sorts of things you should be saying in the meeting itself.

Basics

The first thing to remember is that, while differences exist, the internship interview will almost certainly feel very much like an interview for a full job – and you should treat it as such. If you approach the meeting in a blasé manner and dismiss it as 'just' an internship interview, then the employer will pick up on this very quickly. So always ensure you are in the right mindset from the start of the process. This means all the simple things like not having a couple of drinks with mates the night before, making sure you get a good night's sleep, and spending time preparing what to say (something we will talk about in detail shortly).

Make sure you know how smartly you are expected to dress before the day of the interview. If you are in doubt, email or phone the company in question just to check. Always err on the side of caution and dress slightly more smartly than may be necessary.

---

brilliant tip

The only time you should be wary of being too smart is if you know for a fact the company is very casual (for example some graphic design agencies eschew formal dress completely). Here, being overdressed may count against you, as it could suggest you will not fit into the firm's culture. Otherwise always be a bit smarter than strictly required.

Company dress code	Your interview dress code
Casual	Smart casual – no trainers
Smart casual	Smart – no denim
Suit	Suit and tie

Ensure you know what outfit you want to wear the evening before the interview. It may sound frivolous, but you do not want to be running around looking for your favourite shirt or top on the day of the interview only to find it is in the wash.

On the morning of the interview try not to drink stimulants like coffee or energy drinks. It can be tempting to do so if you feel you need to wake up. However, when you get to the interview you will probably have plenty of adrenalin pumping through your body anyway and any extra caffeine could make you more nervous. Coffee is also a diuretic and can dehydrate you, so drink plenty of water instead and keep your brain hydrated.

Plan how you will get to the interview a day or two beforehand. This is not just a case of checking what train station you need to go to – make sure you know the way from door to door. Print off maps and mark your route, if necessary. You do not want to get in the general vicinity of the company's office and then get stressed walking around trying to work out exactly where it is. Don't be the applicant who has to call up the firm and ask for directions – this is not a good first impression.

Once you have a route planned out and know how long it will take to get there, you should aim to arrive half an hour early. This should give you sufficient breathing space if there are problems on public transport or lots of traffic. Do not, however, go straight in more than 10 minutes early as this can also be an inconvenience for the company. Have a walk around the block and maybe find a café where you can sit down, drink some water and have a final look through your notes. Far better to be killing time around the corner from the office than stressing on a train because you are going to be five minutes late. If, for whatever reason, you are behind schedule and know you will not make your allotted time, then call ahead and warn the company. This is a basic courtesy and is preferable to just turning up 10 minutes after your interview was due to start. Make sure you are very apologetic on the phone and offer a reason why you are running late.

When you arrive, ensure you greet people with a smile and a firm handshake. If you have some time to spare, politely ask if there is a toilet you can use – make sure you do not get caught short during the interview and also check your appearance.

Competence

If you follow all of the above advice, you will have given yourself a good grounding for the interview. The employer knows you can arrive on time and dress appropriately – and you would be surprised at the number of candidates who fall down on those two simple requirements. You now need to convince your interviewer (or interviewers) you have the ability to undertake the internship.

Practically all interviews feature competency-based questions. These are not designed to catch you out or trick you, they are a chance for you to show what your strengths are by giving examples from things you have already done. If you were applying for a permanent job, then the interviewer would expect these examples to come largely from a professional context. However, for internship interviews you can use a far broader range of situations, including academic and extra-curricular.

Before the interview you should sit down and, much like you would with an application, list the qualities the company are looking for in their new intern. You should then make notes of when you have previously demonstrated these qualities, if possible with some facts and figures to back them up. If you were president of a club at university, say how many people were in the club. If you were trusted with cashing up in your summer job, say what sorts of sums you were responsible for.

You may well face fewer competency questions than in a full job interview, as the employer will know that your professional experience will be limited. Instead they are looking for potential and interest in the position, as we shall now see.

Enthusiasm

Perhaps the most important part of your internship interview is demonstrating a genuine interest and enthusiasm for the role and the sector to which you have applied. As we have already seen, when relevant professional experience is less applicable, employers will look more to how interested and enthusiastic you are about the internship. The less experience you have or are required to have, the more important your overall attitude becomes.

A few days before the interview, have another look at the research you did before your initial application. Reacquaint yourself with everything to do with the available position. Make sure you have a solid understanding of what it involves on a day-to-day basis. If you are unsure, try to talk to someone you know who may have knowledge of the particular area. Make sure you are up to date with news from both the company and the sector as a whole.

brilliant tip

It may have been a few weeks (if not months) since you initially applied, so do not rest on your laurels and presume what was current then is still relevant. Go back to the same news sources and check what the main stories have been for the past week or two.

Always remember: employers are not looking for interns who are the finished product or who come with bags of relevant experience. They are looking for people with potential and a genuine interest in what they do. One of the best ways to demonstrate both of these things is to have thoroughly researched everything to do with the position.

Employers will be looking not just for the potential itself but whether you will be able to develop it. You need to be able to show your interviewer that you are willing to learn, able to do so quickly, and not afraid of a hard day's work. If you are asked about something you are unsure of, do not be afraid to admit it. Far better to be truthful about your knowledge than try to bluff your way through a question. Try to turn any admission around by stating this is something you were hoping to learn more about during the placement.

You should get the chance to ask questions during the interview, either over the course of your conversation or after the interviewer has finished questioning you. This is another chance to show off your interest and inquisitiveness. Come prepared with a list of pertinent things to ask about the company and the role.

Asking what direction the business hopes to take in the coming years and clarifying anything you have read about it are both good starts.

 recap

● Plan what you want to wear and the route you will take to the interview at least a day beforehand.

● Arrive punctually – do your level best not to be late. If you are very early, try killing some time by walking around the block or popping into a café.

● Prepare answers to competency questions that are relevant to the internship.

● Demonstrate enthusiasm through research, a willingness to learn, and questions of your own.

PART 2

During your internship

So, all your hard work has paid off and you have landed yourself an internship. Brilliant! This could be the start of something special. This section of the book will help you make the most of this opportunity, from coping with your first day to advice on networking.

There is one thing you should constantly bear in mind throughout your placement: you get out of an internship only what you put in. Don't end up being the intern who sits in the corner waiting to get noticed, sulking because no one is talking to them. An internship is all about being proactive; in the coming pages we will see the best ways to maximise your time at a company.

CHAPTER 8

Preparations and expectations

efore your internship even gets under way in earnest, there are plenty of things you can do to lay the groundwork for a successful placement. This chapter will examine all the preparation work that can be done to ensure your placement gets off on the right foot, and will try to give you an idea of what sorts of things to expect.

Research

Having spent hours in front of a computer looking at what seemed like thousands of different companies and then spent another lifetime trawling through in even greater depth those that gave you an interview, I bet you are pretty fed up with researching businesses. If so, I apologise for the following piece of advice: before starting your internship, do some more research on your host company. It may sound dull and tedious, but nevertheless it is worth acting on.

For the interview you will have built a good picture of the firm as an outsider. That is still useful, but now you have something of an inside track on where you will be working it is valuable to have a more in-depth look at the business. For example, you should know by now who will be directly responsible for you, and what their job title is. Google the person to see if any useful information about them is available online, and try to locate their profile on our old friend LinkedIn. This is not so that you can quote your new boss's entire employment history back at them, but simply so that you have an idea of their own professional strengths and, consequentially, what sort of tasks you might be assisting with. If your interviewer offered some information on the company you were previously unaware of, use this to guide some more focused research into its work and background.

You might also want to ask whoever is in charge of you whether there is anything specific you should read or find out about before starting. They might think of something that will ensure you hit the ground running on your first day.

Dress code

Regardless of whether you are the kind of person who lays out their outfit for the next day before they go to bed or the person who takes the 'pick up something vaguely clean off the floor' approach, it is important to establish the dress code in your new workplace before your first day.

Your interview should have given you a good idea of what kind of clothes will be deemed acceptable for your internship. Similarly, you should be able to make an educated guess from the type of business where you will be working. Offices operating in one of the traditional professions (law, accountancy, etc.) usually will require a suit and shirt, while a graphic design firm is likely to be far more welcoming of denim and a t-shirt. It is, however, always best to ask for specific guidance, as every company is different.

brilliant tip

If you are in any doubt, it is far better to be over-dressed than under-dressed. You'll never get in trouble for wearing a jacket; you might for wearing trainers.

Once you have established the basic dress code, there are a few more variables that are worth bearing in mind. Lots of offices that operate smarter dress codes allow their employees to indulge in 'dress down Friday'. In effect, this means you can ditch the suit and tie and sport your favourite pair of jeans once a week, so you should ask if your host company does anything similar. If you don't realise, it's not the end of the world, but I guess you would probably rather not be the office equivalent of a kid in school uniform on home clothes day ...

More importantly, you should also check if the business has a different dress code for meetings with clients. Companies will often dress up more if they have important meetings, so it is crucial you are prepared for this if you are to accompany your colleagues. It is even worth asking whether you should keep a spare shirt and tie in the office, just in case.

Enquiring about the finer details of dress etiquette can probably wait until you actually start. You don't want to inundate your future manager with questions before you have even got to your desk for the first time. Nevertheless, once you get going, it is valuable to be fully briefed on what and what not to wear during your internship.

What to bring with you

Something many new interns overlook when starting is whether they need to provide anything themselves. In most cases, the company will have everything you would need, but it is worth checking and also bringing some basics with you.

For example, you would be surprised at the number of businesses that have a chronic shortage of pens. You don't really want to be in a situation on your first day where you have to borrow your colleague's prized writing implement every 10 minutes, so bring 1 or 2 of your own.

You will need something to write on too. Again, the majority of workplaces will have notepads for their employees, but, just in case, bring along your own. It is a terrible feeling being in a meeting or listening to careful instructions and not being able to jot them down, so pack your own writing pad to go with your pens. Take the pad everywhere you go as well – you never know when you will need to scribble down a piece of information. Try to make sure it is a fresh one, or certainly one that does not contain anything embarrassing. Your favourite *Winnie the Pooh* booklet is likely to raise a few eyebrows in an office, as will the notepad from university on which your friend scribbled obscene and hilarious phrases.

brilliant tip

It is always a good idea to have a dedicated diary for your internship, and I would suggest purchasing one before you start. Take it to work every day and note down any meetings, appointments or deadlines that you have. More than this, however, you should keep it with you and make notes of all the things you do during your placement. Include specific tasks you did or pieces of work you produced. This will become a very important tool after your internship, as you will see in Part 3.

It is rare, but some businesses may require you to bring in your own laptop, particularly smaller firms that are short of computers. If this is the case, they will, almost certainly, let you know beforehand, but just be aware that this happens occasionally.

Finally, it may sound very simple but, if you are going to be at your desk for most of the day, consider taking in a snack with you. Lots of people forget and end up getting really peckish – and you do not want to be running out of the office halfway through the day to satiate your chocolate craving. Don't forget to check it is OK to eat at your desk before you do so.

Office hours and first day arrival

When preparing to go in for your first day, make sure you are aware of what normal office hours are, and what time you are expected to arrive on your first day.

Never assume your new workplace will operate a classic 9–5 policy, nor should you try to second guess what the working hours might be. Get a clear answer before you start of when you need to arrive every morning for your internship. Plenty of offices prefer to start later than 9 am and, thus, also end later; some will operate flexitime, where you simply have to complete your allotted hours at any time that fits. In all likelihood flexitime will not be an option while you intern, but it is worth checking in case your mentor, boss, or colleagues will be in at different times than those that you might expect.

Often a company will ask you to come in a little later on your first day than you would normally. This is to allow people in the office to get settled and ensure they can spend time with you on your arrival rather than making you wait around while they settle in for the day. Sometimes (particularly for shorter internships and those where your tasks can change on a daily basis) you may be asked to come in a bit later than everyone else every day. Again, do not be put out – this is to ensure your line manager can have tasks prepared for you to save you waiting around.

Managing expectations

It is very important to head into your internship with the right mindset. Hopefully, this book will give you a good idea of what you should and should not expect to come across during an internship, and it is vital that you adopt a level-headed approach to the placement.

Internships are important, but it is a mistake to head into one thinking it is the be-all and end-all of your fledgling career. A good placement may well kick-start your professional life, but it can be just as useful to discover that a certain job or industry is not right for you. So do not panic if things are not going quite as you had hoped, that is all part of the internship learning experience.

Conversely, do not stroll into an internship with a very blasé attitude. It is counter-productive to dismiss an internship as insignificant and temporary when, in reality, it can be a very solid grounding for your future career. If you do have such an offhand manner it will swiftly become obvious to your employer who in turn will commit less time and effort to your training and even cut short your time there. The key is to achieve a balance between having real commitment and being aware that an internship can be helpful, even if it is not quite what you had hoped for or expected.

In a similar vein, do not be tempted to make a snap judgement on the placement, positive or negative. First days are notoriously disappointing as you are forced to go through various bits of admin and bureaucracy. Health and safety talks, setting up a new computer log-in, getting a tour of the office – these are not things you will be forced to do on a daily basis, but will contrive to make the first day of your internship fairly tedious. So do not be tricked into thinking you have signed up to a boring, monotonous placement – just give it some time.

Often you will find it can take a few days, or even a week, before you can really get stuck in. If this is the case, just bide your time and be happy in the knowledge that better times are likely to be just around the corner. Of course, if you continue to be disappointed with your internship beyond a week or two then you should talk to your boss or your mentor about your issues. Of course, you may have an incredible first day, getting thrown straight into what you wanted to be doing and learning huge amounts along the way. Your firm has clearly demonstrated that it already trusts your ability, which is fantastic, but just be aware that there will be some days with more mundane tasks. Regardless of whether your first day (or first week) is brilliant, disappointing, or average, just remember it is only the tip of the iceberg – there is lots more to come.

brilliant tip

Do not expect your first week to be the highlight of your internship. The first few days of any new position inevitably are dominated by administrative procedures and the general process of settling in. This is particularly true of internships, where your company may have to spend some time establishing what level of tasks you are able to complete. So, if you are feeling a little disappointed after the first few days, don't worry!

In your first week or two your company may want to get a clearer picture of how much you already know about your internship area and how well you can work independently. Often this manifests itself in the form of tasks that will allow them to establish the sorts of things they need to teach you, and also to get an idea of your work ethic. If you find these tasks to be a little boring, or indeed too difficult, do not start complaining immediately. There is naturally a period at the start of any internship where the host company will need to work out the professional level of their intern. It is only if the company has not managed to pitch your tasks at the right kind of level after two or three weeks that you should start getting concerned and try to speak to someone.

Finally, don't forget that you are not only the newest person in the company but also the least important from an operational point of view. So do not be surprised if sometimes you have quiet periods where you do not have a huge amount to be getting on with. If this happens, do not be afraid to ask for things to do: the people above you will have plenty of their own work to be getting on with and cannot think of things for you to do all the time. Even if you intern at a company that has devised a very clear and well thought-out internship programme, sometimes you may need to give colleagues a gentle nudge and ask if you can help with anything. This goes a long way in terms of demonstrating enthusiasm and dedication too.

 brilliant recap

- Supplement the reading you did for your interview with more in-depth research.

- Make sure you know the dress code for your first day, and check the finer details after you have started.

- Pack pens, a notepad and, if required, your laptop. Don't forget a snack in case you get peckish.

- Keep an open mind about your internship beforehand and during the first few days. If it is a little disappointing, don't forget it is likely to improve!

CHAPTER 9

Your first day

So, with the internship in the bag and all your meticulous preparations complete, it is time to actually kick things off. If you are feeling a bit nervous, don't worry. It is only natural and, I promise you, everyone else feels the same when they start a new internship. If you have prepared thoroughly, you will be more than ready to get going and, even if you feel under-prepared, do not panic – just be positive.

This chapter will try to give you a rough idea of what your first day will be like and what sorts of treats will be in store. Obviously, every internship is different, but you can expect at least some of the elements we will look at to feature in some order.

Getting there

This section could perhaps have sneaked into the 'Preparations and expectations' chapter, but do make sure you have a very good idea of where you are heading on your first day. Leave plenty of extra time than you would normally to allow for the vagaries of public transport (or traffic if you are driving) and just in case you take any wrong turns on the way to your new work-place. Make sure you know the route you need and do not leave it till you get in the vicinity of the office to start thinking about what number you need to look for or what end of the street it might be. It is certainly advisable to take a map with you as well, regardless of how good you think your sense of direction is.

brilliant tip

If you have the time, it can be a good idea to do a 'trial run' of the commute before you start just to familiarise yourself with the route and to get a good idea of how long the journey will take you. You will be very grateful on your first morning, when you may be feeling a bit stressed, to be retracing steps that you have already taken. You could also discover the website that gave you an estimated time for the trip was not desperately accurate, again saving you a panic on your first morning.

Meeting your colleagues

Having made it safely to the first day of your internship, one of the first things you will do is meet your new colleagues. It can be a bit overwhelming to meet a group of people all at once, but just try to remember the basics. A smile, good eye contact and a firm handshake will all contribute to creating a good first impression.

Don't panic if you cannot remember everyone's names, particularly if you have met more than two or three people at once. You will not be expected to remember everyone on the first go, and no one will mind if you have to re-introduce yourself at a later stage with a polite apology. If you are struggling, focus on remembering your boss and those people you will be working with most closely.

brilliant tip

When trying to remember names, repeat them out loud, confirming to the person you have just met that you have understood them correctly. It will help them stick in your mind. Also, try creating a very quick floor plan of the office and label each desk with the relevant person's name. It is not only useful for referring to in your first few weeks when you have forgotten what someone is called or where they sit, but it will also help cement the names in your mind.

Health and safety

Every company should give you an introduction to their health and safety policy at the start of your internship. This will be one of the things that really doesn't differ for interns or permanent members of staff: anyone who spends time in the company's workplace will be subject to the same introduction. The extent of the health and safety welcome will vary from business to business and often will depend on the nature of the workplace. Clearly there will be far less to go over in an office than in a film studio or a workshop.

Whatever health and safety briefing you have on your first day, make sure you give it your full and proper attention. It may be a bit tedious (let's face it, when is health and safety anything but?), but it will be a legal requirement that you have a proper induction, so do not try to get out of it or ask if you can skip it.

Larger companies may well have a dedicated health and safety officer who will take you through all the aspects of their policy and may even require you to complete a short test to check you understood it all. Don't worry if this is the case: no one is looking to catch you out and the answers to the questions are almost certainly as obvious as you think they are. If you are in a smaller company, a normal employee probably will be the elected health and safety official and you are unlikely to have to do a dedicated test, but still give the health and safety briefing your full attention.

Tour of the workplace

Depending on the size of your company, the tour of your new workplace might be a 30-second stroll around a modestly sized office or it could be a half-hour walk around various departments and even different buildings. If it is the former, you should have little difficulty remembering where everything is. If it is the latter, you may need a few days before you really know where everything is and where you are going.

> **brilliant timesaver**
>
> Don't worry if you can't remember how to get somewhere. If you ask someone politely, they should be more than willing to help out. If you are in a big building and you get completely lost, just head for the main entrance, which will be well sign-posted. There you can ask at reception for help.

When trying to memorise the locations of different parts of the building, start with the most important first. Get a good idea of where your workstation is in relation to other 'landmarks' – stairways, water coolers, etc. – so that you do not get lost every time you have to step away from your desk. It is also very useful to make a mental note of where the nearest toilets are located, and where to find the canteen or kitchen. You should also attempt to remember roughly where you can find colleagues you will be working with if they are not sitting nearby.

Your workstation

During your internship you will, almost certainly, be allocated your own desk or workstation. What this consists of will vary from business to business, but, essentially, this will be where you are likely to spend most of your internship.

On your first day you will probably need to get a user name and password so you can log onto the company system. You may be given a generic temporary one to use, or the company may set up a full account for you. This will depend largely on how long you are staying (or perhaps how efficient the IT department is), so do not be offended if you do not get a personal log-in: it is not a slight on you.

Make sure that the person initiating you shows you all the software on the computer that you will need during your internship. Some of it may be straightforward – for example you may already be comfortable using the Microsoft Outlook email client – but some of it may be completely new to you. If so, make sure you make plenty of notes when processes are explained to you. Forgetting the odd thing is no crime, but it will reflect badly on you if you have to ask for someone to show you how things work three or four times.

brilliant tip

Make sure you check where you can and can't save your work. Sometimes a computer will be set up to erase everything from the desktop or 'My Documents' every time it is shut down, so ensure you do not lose hours of work by knowing where it is safe to save it. This is something that catches many interns out and can be hugely frustrating. If in doubt, email the work to yourself, then you know it is safe.

Finally, double-check whether there are any rules governing what you can and can't do at your desk. The majority of companies are happy for staff and interns to eat and drink at their workstation, but some may ask you to go elsewhere. This is particularly true if you are interning somewhere with lots of valuable equipment where crumbs and spills become that much more serious.

Lunch arrangements

If you are not given specific instructions about lunch arrangements, do not be afraid to ask. You need to find out if there is a specific time you should take your break, and how long you get. Most companies will be pretty flexible about when people can go and eat, although some will try to stagger things so that not everyone is away from the office at the same time. As an intern, you should have pretty flexible eating arrangements, but it is always good to check first.

On your first day you should try to get an idea of what the company's 'lunch culture' is. For example, at some firms employees will spend their entire hour at their desk with a packed lunch. At others, groups of employees may go out for lunch together every day. It is generally a good idea in your first week to do as your colleagues do, particularly as it gives you a good chance to get to know them a bit better. However, if you find all your colleagues stay in the office every lunch break, after a week or so of your internship I would suggest popping out for a quick walk during your break. It will split up the day and help keep your mind fresh.

End of the day

At the end of your first day you will need to clarify whether someone needs to make an official note of your departure or whether you are just free to get up and leave. Hopefully you won't have been clock-watching all afternoon, so you will be pleasantly surprised when the end of the day approaches. You should already know what the office hours are, so, when you reach the allotted finishing time, keep an eye on what your colleagues are doing. If they all start clearing away their things and getting their coats on, then just quickly check with your line manager that you can leave and you are free to go. If no one appears to be leaving, diplomatically check with your boss what time you are meant to stay until. They should then say you can go. Ideally, your boss will be aware that it is time for you to go and will pre-empt you having to ask. However, they will often get side-tracked by something else, so do go and ask. Do not start shutting down your computer and getting your coat on as a way of dropping hints to those around you that you are ready to leave!

Before going, ask whether you can just leave at the same time every day or whether you need to wait for confirmation that you can go. Normally, you will be free to leave as you like, although I would still recommend seeking out your boss to say goodbye before you disappear. This is a matter of courtesy as much as it is a practicality.

You should also double-check your start time for the next day. As we saw earlier, the first day of an internship may be slightly different to the remainder, so it is worth making absolutely sure you know when to arrive.

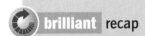 **brilliant** recap

- Allow extra time to get to your internship on your first day and make sure you know the route, perhaps having done a trial run beforehand.

- Remember the basics when meeting colleagues: smile, eye contact, firm handshake.

- Don't panic if you can't remember everyone's names.

- Try making a rough floor plan of the office with people's names by their desks: it will come in very handy.

- If you are in a large office, focus on remembering where your desk is in relation to essential spots such as toilets and kitchen/canteen.

- Make full notes when being taken through tasks and processes.

- Check lunch arrangements, including whether you can eat at your desk.

- At the end of the day check your boss is happy for you to go and whether there is any formal system for departing.

CHAPTER 10

Your mentor

E very good internship should allocate a mentor to the interm. What format this takes, from how formal the set-up is to which staff member has the responsibility, will vary from company to company and internship to internship. This chapter will give you some guidance on what sorts of things you should expect from your mentor, what sorts of things you should talk about with them, and what falls outside of their remit.

Purpose

A dedicated mentor during your internship primarily will help deal with two areas. Firstly, they will oversee personal progression and education during the internship. Secondly, they will be your first port of call should any issues arise over the course of your placement.

Before you start your internship your host company should have outlined learning objectives for the placement. This simply may be several bullet points covering areas where you will develop greater professional knowledge, or it could be several paragraphs with specific targets and goals for you to attain. It is your mentor's job to ensure your internship is providing you with the training that will help you achieve these goals, and to check that you feel that you are progressing in the role as well as you had hoped.

If any problems appear over the course of your internship, it is the job of your mentor to liaise with you and the relevant parties within the company to ensure these are resolved to the satisfaction of everyone involved. You should be able to approach your mentor at any point when you have an issue or something you want clarified – they are, essentially, your safety net within the firm.

Formats

As I have already intimated, the format the mentorship will take will depend largely on the size and nature of the company. In larger businesses you probably will find a more formal mentor system in place. This could include weekly or fortnightly meetings with your mentor to discuss in detail how you feel your internship is progressing and any other relevant things you would like to talk about. Your mentor might, in conjunction with your line manager, also conduct monthly reviews into your performance. This will include areas in which you have done well and areas the company feels you could benefit from working on. Your mentor is also likely to pass on more general feedback from your team to you, either face to face or via email.

In smaller firms the mentorship is likely to be less rigid in nature. You may not have meetings scheduled every single week and the passing on of feedback may well have a less systematic structure. That is not to say that mentoring in smaller companies is necessarily of a lower standard. Rather you probably will receive a steadier stream of information and help from your mentor than occasional in-depth conversations at timetabled meetings.

brilliant tip

If you find that you do not have many official meetings with your mentor and would like some more structured feedback, then do ask for more frequent conversations. As long as you are not unreasonable in your requests – do not expect a daily briefing – your mentor should be more than happy to oblige.

You will also find the size of your company may affect which staff member becomes your mentor. In larger companies, often you will be allocated a mentor who works for a completely different department to the one in which you are interning. In smaller companies your line manager normally will also act as your mentor for the internship.

The former allows the mentor greater independence. He or she will be less involved with your day-to-day work, so can take a broader view of your internship and offer you some advice without worrying about how it will affect your day-to-day working relationship.

The advantage of the latter is that it does not rely on formal channels of communication for feedback and advice to reach the intern. You will hear directly from those you work with about the things you are doing well and the things that you can improve.

Issues you should raise

There are some things that you should always raise with your mentor if you are unhappy with them during your internship. If you feel you are not learning enough from the work you are doing, you certainly should talk to your mentor about this. An internship, particularly if you are not being paid, should be a chance to gain a greater understanding and knowledge of a certain area of work. So, if you feel the tasks you are being set are not helping you develop, or you are not being given enough support with those tasks, then you should mention this.

The same is true of the opposite situation: if you feel you are consistently being given too much information and you are struggling to take it all in, then you should tell your mentor. It is far better for both you and the company if the pace of your internship is one you are comfortable with. That way you will get the most out of the experience, and the firm will know you are happy with what you are doing.

 **example**

You have offered to stay late one evening to complete an urgent task. You end up having to stay late every day for a week to work on various projects.

This is certainly something to talk to a mentor about – as an intern it should not be your responsibility to work regularly beyond your set hours. You need to find a balance between showing commitment and avoiding being exploited.

If the tasks you are set do not match your expectations in terms of learning outcomes and the stated purpose of the internship, you should also raise this with your mentor. An internship is not like a permanent job where often you will have to demonstrate plenty of flexibility – the employer has a responsibility to keep an intern's work centred on the main focus of the internship. If this is not happening you should say so.

If you find you have a personal issue with a colleague – perhaps you do not get on, or have found them unwelcoming and difficult – it can also be worth mentioning this to your mentor. Naturally you should do so subtly and confidentially, but it is worth doing to see if the problem can be resolved. It is rare for this to happen, of course, but, if it does occur for whatever reason, it is best to talk to someone about it.

If, during the course of your internship, a personal issue arises that could affect your work, it is always best to tell your mentor. They can offer support and ensure that, if you need some time off or extra help with tasks, you can receive this without any difficulties.

Very occasionally you may find that a company's accounts department has not been as efficient as you had hoped, and you find you are owed money for wages or expenses. Again, it is good practice to raise this with your mentor first and they can take appropriate action to ensure you get what you are due. It is far better to do this than complain directly to the finance team who may deal only with more senior staff members.

Things not to mention

You should also exercise some discretion when talking to your mentor – there are some things that are neither appropriate nor wise to mention to them. You should avoid bringing up personal issues that do not affect your work or have a major impact on your general disposition. Your mentor will not want to hear whether you met an attractive member of the opposite sex at the weekend, nor if your parents have just booked a nice family holiday to Spain (unless of course it requires you to take time off, or you are really struggling for small talk!).

brilliant tip

Meeting with a mentor is not a forum for spreading or trying to find out about office gossip. Even if you are convinced your mentor would love to hear about the two colleagues in the photocopy room, I suggest keeping quiet. Spreading rumours and tittle-tattle does not reflect well on you, or your professional demeanour.

Minor work problems that are very easily resolved are also best avoided. Needing a new notepad or pen, for example, is something your line manager can deal with very quickly. It is not something that a mentor should face. They are there to help with your internship as a whole, not every single detail.

Although it is tempting, try not to keep pestering your mentor about the potential for future work or a job at the end of the internship. It is only really suitable to broach the subject within the last few weeks of your placement and normally the mentor themselves will mention it first. If you do go over the top in your pursuit of employment after the internship, you will do your chances more harm than good (as frustrating as that may be). For more advice on employment after your internship turn to Part 3.

You should not expect detailed feedback from your mentor on every individual piece of work that you produce for the company. While you may get this in your first few weeks it is unlikely to carry on throughout the internship. It is safe to presume that, if you are not getting detailed feedback for every piece of work you do, then you are doing OK. A mentor is there to provide an overview, not micromanage your output.

brilliant recap

- Your mentor is your main port of call for discussion and feedback relating to your internship.

- The nature of the mentoring will vary from company to company, but every good internship should have one (even informally).

- Talk to your mentor about serious work issues, such as what you are learning and how you are progressing.

- Also raise personal problems if they are affecting your work.

- Do not seek out your mentor to talk about minor information that is not relevant to your development.

CHAPTER 11

Your boss

Over the course of your internship you may well find that you come under the supervision of several different members of staff. Alternatively, you may have one manager who remains constant but you may be assisting different colleagues on different tasks and, as a result, have several different people whom you report to on a day-to-day basis. Whatever set-up you find your internship takes with regards to bosses, this chapter will give you some advice on how to deal with them, what they will expect from you, and how your relationship may differ from that with other colleagues.

Who is your boss?

It may seem like a very obvious question, but be sure you know who your boss is and whether there is more than one. Often, particularly for interns who might end up working on several different projects, you could find yourself answering to two or three different people. It is therefore important to establish what level of seniority these people have and how much responsibility they bear for you and your work.

If you are working on just one project during your internship, or are working within one small department, it should be pretty clear who your boss is. Normally you will find that it is the team leader on your project, or the manager of the department. You should know that they are the person to talk to when work issues crop up, and that, ultimately, they will sign off your work.

Alternatively, you may find that the person in charge of your department has delegated responsibility for you to the colleague with whom you work most closely.

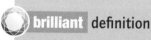

brilliant definition

'Boss'

A boss is, essentially, anyone to whom you report or who takes responsibility for your activities during your internship. Thus you may have several different people whom you regard as 'bosses' over the course of your placement. Normally, however, you will have one manager who has overall control of what you do, even if you report to various members of staff.

(In?)formal relationship

Every boss or manager is different. You will come across a huge array of contrasting characters over the course of your career, some good, some bad. During your internship, as you take your first steps into the world of work, you will need to grow accustomed to handling the occasionally complex nature of a worker–boss relationship.

Normally, your boss will have a quick chat with you in your first week to reiterate what is expected of you during the internship, what you can expect to get out of it, and to give you an idea of how the department or project runs. You should be able to glean some information from this initial conversation on what kind of boss you are dealing with. Try to establish from what they say if they are very hands-on, overseeing every detail in every piece of work produced, or if they are happy to let their team get on with their tasks and prefer to observe from afar. You should be prepared to adjust your working habits accordingly.

This is not to say that, if you have a hands-on boss, you should not worry about time management and let someone else do it for you. Similarly, having a less involved boss does not mean you should not be studious in your note-taking and recording of work. Simply, you should expect that, under different types of bosses, different facets will come under more scrutiny and this should be borne in mind.

brilliant example

If you feel your boss is the very involved type, you can presume that he will check the majority of your work and also oversee how you are spending your time. So you can be ready for this by keeping notes on all the work you have done, how long it has taken you, and what tasks are next on your list of things to do.

Conversely, if the boss appears to be less closely involved with the day-to-day work of his charges, you can also prepare yourself appropriately. You can assume that you will not have someone breathing down your neck all the time, so you can perhaps worry a little less about having perfect records of your work ready to present at any time. However, if you are monitored less, there is far greater onus on you to manage your time appropriately and set yourself realistic targets for the completion of work.

You may also get some useful information on how your boss operates by talking to colleagues. This shouldn't be an excuse for you to crudely ask, 'So what's so-and-so *really* like then?', but there may be an appropriate moment to enquire gently among your co-workers if there is anything particular you should know about the boss. Of course your boss him/herself may offer their own insight into what they are like to work for. This could be very useful but, then again, it might not bear much relation to reality.

Away from overseeing your work, you should try to gain an awareness of what sort of relationship is suitable to build with your boss. In many cases it is prudent to maintain a level of professional distance with your boss – they retain responsibility for you during the internship so it is generally preferable that you do not become too friendly with them. You could accidentally reveal something that it is better for them not to hear, which would leave both of you in an awkward position.

That said, some bosses will actively seek to engage with you on a social level and encourage you to be more friendly with them. While it is still wise to not be overly familiar, it could be considered rude if you do not respond in kind, and developing a more friendly relationship with your boss should help your working relationship. Either way, it is best to follow the example your boss takes. Do not be the one to instigate personal conversations, but do not ignore your boss if they do so.

Disciplinary issues

Before starting, your boss should outline any rules that you are expected to follow (confidentiality, use of work computers, and so on). If you are not given specific instructions on office rules, then simply be sensible and do not do anything you think might be frowned upon. You should not need to be told that turning up late or taking extended lunch breaks are not allowed! There is no reason why you should break any rules during your internship. If you feel particularly strongly that something you are not permitted to do or must do is unreasonable, then gently raise the issue with your boss. However, remember you are there to work, not to have fun, and denying you the chance to check Facebook at your desk is not an unreasonable expectation.

If, for whatever reason, any disciplinary issues do arise, it is almost certainly your boss who will deal with any rule breaking. Depending on the severity of the incident, it may even go further up the chain of command. If you are in the wrong, be apologetic, try to explain what happened, and promise that it will not happen again.

brilliant recap

- Establish who has responsibility for you and your work, remembering this may be more than one person and can change.

- Be aware that different bosses will focus on different skills and require different things from your output.

- Try to maintain a good level of professionalism in your relationship with your manager.

- There should be no reason that you break any office rules but, if you do, offer your boss a contrite apology.

CHAPTER 12

Your colleagues

S o you have got to grips with how to deal with your mentor and you are comfortable facing your boss. Now it is time to talk about your colleagues. Colleagues are a strange breed: you do not pick them, but you spend more time with them than you do your friends or family. They are therefore a central part of your internship and getting on with them can be key to gaining the most benefit from the placement. This chapter will help you build relationships, deal with any problems that arise, and even help you negotiate the minefield of company flings.

Getting to know colleagues

Unlike a shorter period of work experience, an internship normally will last several months, giving you far more time to get to know your colleagues (and making it more important to do so). As an intern, you will be working alongside these people for a not insignificant amount of time, so it is important for you and your new workmates to build positive relationships.

That is not a cue to go in on your first day and tell your new colleagues that you are sure you will all be best friends forever. It takes time to develop positive, constructive relationships, but it is worth doing. Do not make the mistake of thinking that you can put in minimal effort with co-workers as your internship is only temporary. Three months is still a long time when you are spending five days a week with people and, if you are to get the most out of your placement, you will need to be in your colleagues' good books. Moreover, many internships lead to permanent work, so you could end up spending a lot more than three months with these people.

At the start of your internship, the only thing you know you have in common with fellow workers is the fact that you are employed by the same company. It is therefore a good idea to try to establish some other common ground with colleagues on which you can develop some kind of rapport. It is often easiest to make a connection through a shared pastime – if you get an inkling that someone you work with shares one of your passions (be that football, fashion or falconry) then get chatting about it. Suddenly, you are not just the new intern; you are fellow aficionado for a like-minded person to talk with.

If you cannot find an obvious affinity with someone in the office, try to find out more about them. What university did they go to? If you are an alumnus of the same institution you will always have something to talk about. Where do they live? What are their favourite holiday destinations? It may seem daunting at first, but I would be very surprised if you could not find at least one person at your internship who has something in common with you.

You should use breaks in the working day to get to know your co-workers better. Lunch is a great opportunity to get talking to people around you in the office, particularly if you have stepped out for a bite to eat. Away from the workplace you will find people often tend to be a bit more open and friendly. If you are a smoker, you may find that you take a cigarette break with colleagues, again allowing you another chance to strike up conversation in a less formal atmosphere.

Of course the culture in some offices is very much one of all work, no play. If this is the case, do not try to force things with colleagues, they may be uninterested in striking up a rapport with other people in their workplace. Hopefully, you will have done enough research into the company beforehand that you are expecting (and are happy with) this less social set-up.

Asking for help

An important reason for getting on well with your colleagues is that they are the people you work with most closely and inevitably will require help from at some point. This is not something to worry about or be ashamed about. Questions and queries are inevitable for any new member of staff, and even more so from a new intern. Your colleagues should know that you are there to learn and should be forthcoming with any answers or help you need.

However, do not ask about every single minor issue you come across and are not entirely sure about. It is perhaps OK to do so in your first few days as you get settled in, but it will quickly grow frustrating for colleagues and will definitely reflect badly on you. If you can make a reasonable, educated guess at what to do then go with that – you will not get in trouble if you have tried a sensible option, even if it is not the right one. Obviously, if you aware that the question could have a major effect on the task you are doing, then you should be more inclined to ask for help. The main thing is to avoid constantly harassing co-workers with irrelevant and inconsequential queries.

brilliant tip

If the help you require is directly related to the work you are doing, it is usually best to ask the person with whom you are working most closely for that particular task. They will have a good idea already of what you are doing, and are most likely to be able to offer relevant assistance and advice. If you have a more general query about the office or general protocol then feel free to ask the person you find the most friendly, helpful or engaging.

Problems with colleagues

With a bit of luck, you will get on very well with all your colleagues and sail through your internship without any negative
issues cropping up. Unfortunately, there are some rare occasions
where you come across a colleague with whom you do not get on
so well. Always remember that, unless you have been behaving
inappropriately, this isn't your fault and it is just one of those
things. Inevitably, over the course of your professional life, you
will come across people who are not quite your cup of tea. It is
unlucky if this happens on your internship but there are some
things you can do to minimise any potential issues.

The first thing to bear in mind is that, during the first few weeks
of your internship, you will not necessarily strike up an instant
rapport with your new colleagues. It takes time to earn trust and
respect, particularly if you are entering a group that is already
quite close-knit. So do not jump to any conclusions early on in
your placement, give everyone some time to get to know you.

If you find you genuinely do not get on with someone at work,
often the best thing to do is simply to minimise the amount of
contact you have with them. You will have to see them occasionally but, if you stay out of their way as much as possible, that
will do a lot to ease any tensions that might exist. That is not to
say you should avoid them at all costs, but do not try to force
the issue.

If you do find you have to work closely with a less friendly colleague, that is unfortunate, but look at it as a good additional
experience from your internship. The lessons you learn from
it will, undoubtedly, be useful in the future. Remain courteous
and be as nice as you can, without going over the top on false
displays of warmth. You may well get frustrated, but use the
opportunity to grit your teeth and practise some self-restraint.
Generally, try not to antagonise the situation and, hopefully,

everything will run smoothly, even if you do not get on that well with your colleague.

It is also worth remembering that this is an internship and therefore not permanent. At the end of it you can just walk away and forget about the person in question: you are not committed to stay. If your internship goes well, and there is a chance of a job at the end, then you have the option of asking to work on a different project or team away from anyone you do not get on with.

If you feel the issue is worth addressing, for example if you are unsure why a certain colleague has taken a dislike to you, you should raise this with your mentor. They might be able to offer some advice and attempt to defuse the situation, if necessary. If you get on well with other co-workers, you could also try talking to them about it. You will need to be subtle and not just start moaning about someone they might actually like. However, sometimes a colleague may be able to resolve differences or smooth out any misunderstandings better than a mentor or boss.

Very rarely, you may find things get to a stage where you are struggling to continue working alongside someone and it is having a negative impact on your internship as a whole. If the issue cannot be resolved, it is worth considering asking to move onto a different team or to work on a different project. This is a less drastic step than quitting altogether, and means your hard work earning the internship has not been undone.

If you find you have a problem with more than one colleague, particularly if the issue is that you are constantly being excluded or even singled out, then this is definitely something to raise with your mentor. It is entirely unacceptable for employees to pick on anyone, particularly an intern, and the company should have disciplinary procedures in place to deal with anyone who engages in any form of bullying.

Away from the office

You will find that over the course of your internship you have chances to develop your relationship with colleagues away from the office. As I have already suggested, such situations are a great chance to get to know the people you work with better, away from the stresses and strains of their jobs.

brilliant impact

Employers often organise sporadic team-building exercises for their staff, which are designed to foster a sense of team spirit and help colleagues build stronger bonds with one another. The activities can range from go-karting and paintballing to wine tasting and are generally good fun. Usually interns will be included in any 'extra-curricular' events the company arranges. This gives you a great chance to cultivate connections with your co-workers and also lets them see you in a more relaxed atmosphere.

Quite often you will find your colleagues go for drinks after work: this is another chance to get to know them better. If you are asked to join them then it is always best to make the effort to go along – it is not only polite but also you will find it makes integrating within the office a lot easier. And you would be surprised how much easier it is to talk to your boss after he or she has had a few drinks ...

Some companies (particularly larger ones) also run sports teams for their staff, or your colleagues may have set up their own teams together. It is often worth enquiring whether the firm does have an official or unofficial team for any sports you play – for example a lot of staff have netball teams and five-a-side football teams. You can make your interest known and then, if they ever need an extra player, they might call on you. This is another useful avenue for getting to know your workmates better and is also good fun – nothing engenders a good communal spirit like a shared victory (or even defeat).

Flings and relationships

There is always a chance that you get to know your co-workers so well that you become a little *too* attached to a colleague. It is not something to feel guilty about – you are not the first person to fall for a colleague – but it is worth saying up front: this is dangerous territory. The best advice I can give is to avoid any work-based romance entirely, for a number of reasons. Sometimes it does work out OK, but it can also have very serious consequences for both parties involved.

If you do feel you have a strong connection to a colleague and you would like to act on that, do remember that an internship is temporary: you will have only a few months to get through before you are free from the constraints of the office. It is therefore prudent to wait until the placement is over before you do anything. This will avoid any unnecessary conflicts with work.

Of course, if you return to the same company after your internship or are hired permanently straight after the placement, then the same issue could arise. Again, I would advise caution, but there are different dynamics when you are a fully fledged member of staff, so perhaps there is less of a risk.

If you are so smitten with your new beau (or really cannot control your carnal desires), then do your very best to keep the relationship subtle, particularly around your superiors. This means absolutely no public displays of affection in the office, which includes long, adoring looks at each other across the water cooler. If you give them ammunition, people will quickly twig that something is going on.

You should remember that businesses often have specific policies and rules governing inter-company relationships, so simply engaging in one could, potentially, lead to disciplinary action against you. Perhaps, more significantly, there may be stricter procedures in place to deal with staff members who carry on relationships with interns, predominantly to prevent the very occasional isolated cases of employees taking advantage of an intern's desire to secure a full-time job. You should, therefore, be aware of the position you are placing your colleague in and the very serious repercussions that could follow.

 brilliant recap

- Try to find common ground with colleagues.
- Use breaks in the working day to get to know them better.
- Do not be afraid to ask colleagues for help.
- Do not bother them with every single small query you have – take an educated guess if it is not a major issue.
- Remember, it will take a few weeks before you really start getting to know workmates.
- If you have a problem with a colleague, try to stay out of their way.
- If you must work with them, treat it as part of the learning experience – you are developing office politics skills.
- If there is a serious issue with one or more colleagues, do not be afraid to raise it with your mentor.
- Get involved with 'extra-curricular' activities, such as sports, casual drinks and team-building exercises.
- Try to avoid work relationships.
- If you do indulge in one, then keep it subtle.
- Be aware of potential disciplinary issues that a work fling might cause.

CHAPTER 13

Social media and the workplace

The advent of social media has brought with it a whole new range of etiquettes and protocols to consider within a workplace. Social media is a brilliant tool for connecting people and disseminating information: this chapter will help you to use it in a work context without compromising your internship.

Company policy

Your first action should be to establish whether your company operates any specific social media policy with regard to its usage. If you know the rules, you know whether you will be breaking them or not by hopping on Facebook at lunchtime.

If there is official company policy on social media usage, there is a good chance that it will ban any accessing of Facebook, Twitter, etc. This is perfectly normal, and nothing to complain about. In much the same way, you will probably not be allowed to phone friends from the office or connect with them online either. If your company has banned social media, look at it from their point of view – do they really want their staff spending time at work organising their social lives?

If there is no specific mention of social media policy during your induction, or in any of the information you are given, you may first want to make discreet inquiries with a colleague. It is probably not a good idea to ask your boss in your first week if you are allowed to check Facebook during your breaks – it gives the impression you are not interested in doing any work.

If there is no official policy, your colleague or colleagues should be able to give you a good idea of accepted practice. There may be a broad rule for not using the internet for personal purposes, in which case you can assume social media comes under this blanket ban. Conversely, it may be the case that everyone accesses social media websites in the office when they are not working, in which case you can probably assume it will be OK for you to do so, if you spend breaks at your desk. If very few people do it, then you should avoid it too – it is clearly not within the company culture.

Accessing social media at work

Having verified what the office policy or attitude is towards the use of social media at work, you should follow these guidelines closely.

If social media is officially banned, then do not be tempted to try to access it. Many companies will have their IT systems set up not only to block banned websites, but also to note when someone attempts to access one of them. So do not be tempted to see if you can have a cheeky browse when no one is looking, as there is still a good chance someone will know about it. Even if such a system does not exist at your company, you never know who might be looking round your shoulder, or might pop over to your desk unexpectedly. And there is nothing more obvious than an employee frantically trying to hit the 'x' at the top right corner of the screen with a guilty look on their face. It is simply best to toe the line and leave it completely – after all, do you really need to see your friends' status updates that urgently?

If you are officially permitted to use social media during your breaks, then do so sparingly. Answer messages; reply to something on your Facebook wall; but it is usually a good idea not to start browsing photos aimlessly or mindlessly flicking through profiles. Apart from anything else, you may not want your colleagues or boss to spot on your screen what state you were in at 3 am on Saturday night. If you are spending your whole working day at your desk, you will also find it far more beneficial to get up and have a walk around during breaks than continuing to stare at a monitor.

brilliant tip

As a rule of thumb, be very conservative with your personal use of social media at work. Remember why you are in the office in the first place – to learn about a job and do an internship that could provide countless benefits to your career. So, even if social media usage is allowed at work, use it minimally – spend your spare time getting to know colleagues, getting a better idea of the company, going over what you have learnt during the day.

Using social media for commercial purposes

The increasing use of social media by companies for commercial purposes does add a new consideration to social media and the workplace. Where previously Facebook, Twitter, et al. were distrusted and disliked by business, many firms are now warmly embracing them and the marketing/customer relations opportunities they provide.

This means that employees often will need to log in to social media at work in order to do their job properly, a fact that brings with it various complications and temptations. Moreover, many companies (particularly smaller enterprises) are turning to their interns to help develop their social media output. Generally speaking, students and graduates will have been using social media for longer than existing employees and, as such, will have a far better inherent understanding of its capabilities and potential.

If you are asked to do some work on social media during your internship, there are two main things to bear in mind. Firstly and most importantly, you will be representing your firm in a very public sphere. Ensure the content you produce and the tone of voice you use are suitable for the company and its image, particularly if you find that only one or two people check what you have produced before it is sent into the world. If you are ever in doubt, double-check with your boss that your work is OK before publishing. Secondly, there is even greater temptation to quickly check your personal accounts if you are using social media for work. Resist it!

It is worth drawing attention to specific considerations for some of the bigger social networking sites as well. Facebook, for one, sometimes requires slightly awkward arrangements for companies using it. At the time of writing (Facebook is constantly evolving so do not take this as gospel), companies are not allowed to have their own Facebook account, they can have only a Page. That means an individual will have to use their own private account to set up and administer a company Facebook Page. Once they have set up a Page, you have the option of using Facebook as the Page itself, to 'like' or post something, for example. However, you will still need a personal log-in. On a practical level, that will mean your company will have to make you an administrator, or a colleague will have to let you use their Facebook log-in if you are to work on the site. Such procedures do not make the separation of personal social media and work very easy, but it is something you may have to learn to cope with.

brilliant tip

If you have been using social media for work purposes, make sure you log out after you have finished. You do not want to get confused between the two. For example, you don't want to post an irrelevant work tweet on your account and, even worse, you do not want the ridiculous video of a dog on a skateboard you just watched to find its way onto your work's timeline.

There are no such problems with Twitter – any person or organisation is allowed to have an account within the normal terms and conditions. If you have your own Twitter account, you may be asked to state in your 'Bio' that you are an intern at your company, or your company may link to your account in their Twitter Bio or one of their Lists. This practice is carried out as it is widely accepted that being able to show the human face of a company has numerous marketing benefits. If you are very uncomfortable with the idea of being one of the 'faces' of your firm, then you can ask politely if you can be exempted. If you have no major issue with the idea, it might mean that you get yourself a handful of new followers and a few more retweets. However, it also means that there will be people viewing your 140-character musings in the context of you as an employee, so you should be careful not to say anything too controversial or expletive-laden. Always wondered why people have the 'all views stated are my own and not those of my employer' bit in their Bios? Now you know. It does not mean you have to really hold back on Twitter, just remember it is a far more public forum than Facebook. Always distinguish between Facebook status updates, designed for selected friends, and tweets, open to everyone. If you find yourself interchanging between personal and work Twitter accounts in the office, then always double-check you are logged in as who you think you are before posting anything.

Finally, a quick word on LinkedIn. It is fair to say that the majority of students and graduates do not use LinkedIn until they have found their first job. If you have not signed up to LinkedIn before starting your internship, something this book recommended in Chapter 2, then now is definitely the time to do it. Indeed, your company may suggest or even insist you do. Most people you come across in business will now have a look at your LinkedIn profile before or after they meet you, and it is a great place to cement new contacts. Once you start building up your contacts list (remember they can be friends and family too), your overall network will grow and you will be able to reach a larger number of people, some of whom may even be useful to your internship or to your company. Most importantly, it is great for connecting with colleagues, as we will see shortly.

'Friending' colleagues

In years gone by, the biggest social questions surrounding new colleagues might have revolved around who to sit next to at lunch or whether to go for drinks with a workmate. There is now the whole new realm of social media to contend with when dealing with those around you in the office.

Like most things we have discussed already regarding social media, the best policy when using it with colleagues is to be cautious and conservative. There are also different considerations for different platforms, so let's have a look at the three major ones individually.

Facebook

Facebook is, primarily, a place to stay in touch with friends and family. This is something to bear in mind when deciding whether to extend a friend request to colleagues. There is a good chance that your colleagues will want to keep their work and social lives separate so, even if you get on well with someone in the office, it does not necessarily mean you should add them on Facebook. You are first and foremost colleagues, not friends. It may sound a bit cold, but this is often the way offices operate. The best policy as a junior member of staff is to wait and see if workmates start adding you on Facebook. If a colleague sends *you* an unwanted friend request then do not feel you have to accept it – you have as much right as they do to keep your work and social lives separate. Alternatively, you can accept it and adjust your privacy setting accordingly, something we discuss shortly.

Twitter

Given Twitter is an open platform, it is not unreasonable to start following colleagues if you find their tweets interesting. If your internship involves working with Twitter, you may be encouraged to do so. You should not necessarily go looking for your colleagues on Twitter straight away but, if you do come across their profiles, then do not feel you need to be as reticent as on Facebook. If you find a co-worker on Twitter who protects their tweets, I would advise being less forward, though. If tweets are protected, it usually means they are just for family or friends, so Facebook-style rules apply for adding them.

LinkedIn

As we have seen, LinkedIn is a professional social networking tool, so should be treated differently from both Facebook and Twitter. It is good practice to 'connect' with anyone you have dealings with in a work context, and that includes your colleagues. It is therefore not unreasonable to add your colleagues within the first week of your internship. You should remember, though, that LinkedIn is for commercial purposes, not social. It is therefore not good practice to add people on LinkedIn and start treating it like Facebook by messaging people for non-work related issues.

☀ **brilliant** tips

When friending colleagues on social media there are almost three degrees of 'socialness'.

1 **Facebook**. This is just for friends and family, and workmates do not necessarily equal friends. So, as a rule of thumb, hold back from sending friend requests to colleagues.

2 **Twitter**. It is a public forum, and it is therefore not unreasonable to follow colleagues whom you come across. But do not go out of your way to find everyone you work with on the site.

3 **LinkedIn**. It is designed specifically for use with work, and you should be active in connecting with colleagues on the site.

Privacy settings

When doing an internship it is good practice to check that the privacy settings on your social media accounts are set up as you would like and no one uninvited can see anything you want kept private. Best practice governing what should be on display, and to whom, varies a large amount depending on the social network and, again, we will look at each of the big three in detail.

The biggest minefield, in terms of protecting who can see what, is Facebook. The world's largest social network has come in for criticism for making its privacy controls difficult and unclear, so you should take care to ensure you know exactly what parts of your profile are on public display, if at all.

It is probably wise to hide all parts of your profile, other than your profile picture, from non-friends to ensure no one you work with at your internship can see anything embarrassing or compromising. That includes friends of friends: you never know what random connections you might have to new colleagues. If your profile picture itself does not portray you in the most professional light, it could be worth hiding that too. If you are being very cautious, or do not want to have anyone from work even finding you on Facebook, you can hide your profile entirely.

If you do become friends with colleagues on Facebook, you can still control what they can and cannot see. By setting up a 'friend list' and putting any colleagues in there you can then filter what information they can access from your profile. So, if you post a harmless update about seeing a film, then they can see it, while anything you would rather they did not see – such as holiday photos – remains behind closed doors, so to speak.

On Twitter you essentially have two privacy settings: private and public. You either protect your tweets so that only approved people can see them, or you let everyone see what you are saying. The former is really useful only if you use Twitter predominantly to communicate with friends rather than interacting with the wider world (which is its main strength). If you are on Twitter, my suggestion is to keep your tweets public, but to exercise some caution when posting things that might not reflect well on you in a work context. If you do want to show friends something a little improper, then you can send them a Direct Message (DM), or even use Facebook.

Finding the right balance on LinkedIn between protecting your privacy and allowing potentially useful contacts to find you is less clear cut than on other social networks. There are some LinkedIn users who allow absolutely everyone to see them and are happy to connect with anyone who invites them. Colloquially, they are known as LIONs – LinkedIn Open Networkers. Conversely, there are some people who will allow only people in their immediate network to contact them, particularly those higher up in companies. When you are starting your career, it is generally a good idea to be as open as possible to new contacts. You never know who will look at your profile and get in touch, so do not make your profile off-limits.

Watching what you say on social media

Having adjusted your privacy settings to a desired level, you should now be confident that colleagues and your superiors at work will not see anything you do not want them to. However, you should still be wary about what you say on social media generally – you never know who it might get back to.

brilliant example

You do not get on well with your boss. Instead of discussing your grievances in private with a mentor or colleague, you decide to moan about him or her on Twitter. One of your team happens to find your profile, and sees the tweet. You are now facing disciplinary action, or possibly an early termination of your internship.

So, if you do feel the need to let off a little steam about any aspect of your internship, do it in a private way – a Facebook message to a friend or a text perhaps. Do not air your grievances in public!

When you start your internship, and thus your professional life, you need to start thinking of social media as a type of personal PR. It allows you to project an image of yourself to the world and, whether you like it or not, some of that image will be picked up by your company. Watching what you say on social media is, therefore, not just avoiding the obvious such as moaning about colleagues or your placement. It means that you should start thinking about everything that you post online through a professional filter. How will this reflect on me during my internship? What will a potential employer think of this? Will my colleagues mind me saying this? Only on stuff that you know is absolutely private – such as Facebook messages – should you feel free to let your guard down. Remember, many people have hundreds of 'friends' on Facebook, many of whom you do not really know that well. As a rule of thumb, if you do not want people to see something, do not post it publicly.

 **brilliant** recap

- Establish your company's social media policy for staff. If there isn't one, find out what the norm is for your colleagues.
- Stick to the rules! Don't be tempted to have a cheeky look at Facebook if it is banned.
- Be careful not to confuse personal accounts and work accounts.
- Do not attempt to add all your colleagues as social media 'friends', but do consider connecting with them on LinkedIn.
- Double-check your privacy settings and ensure you have hidden sensitive parts of your social media profiles.
- Be careful what you say on social media – it is a public sphere. Think of your online presence as your own brand and PR.

CHAPTER 14

Day-to-day office life

Your learning experience on an internship is limited not just to gaining insights into a particular role or sector. There are many different things that you will have to deal with on a daily basis, varying from the functional (e.g. emails) to the mundane (e.g. getting coffee), which many interns are unsure of before they start their placement. It may sound trivial but, having a grasp of how to perform basic office functions, such as using a photocopier, will greatly improve your ability to do your work. An internship is a great way of learning these things before starting your first job. This chapter will give you an idea of what to expect in the course of day-to-day office life and help prepare you for it.

Email

As you might expect, email is the most regular form of communication used in the workplace. While I am sure you already use email regularly and are comfortable with its basic functions, using it in a professional context throws up a number of new considerations that you may not have faced previously.

The tone of voice and level of formality used in emails is one area where interns often make mistakes. It is hugely important to remember that sending a quick message to a friend is very different from sending one to a colleague and, in turn, that can be very different from sending an email to a client. When you message a friend, you probably use abbreviations, colloquial language and intimate greetings without even thinking about it. Such slangy communication is generally not acceptable in a work context and, as such, you will have to take care to ensure the emails you send during an internship use formal language. It may sound tedious but not doing so will have a negative impact on your placement. That could be anything from colleagues thinking less of your work, to damaging a client relationship.

---

brilliant example

Below are two emails, saying much the same thing, but one using colloquial language and the other more formal. They are slightly exaggerated for emphasis, but contain a number of common mistakes interns often make in their emails. Look out, in particular, for punctuation, capitalisation, abbreviations and colloquial expressions.

gary

Cheers for your message got it yesterday. yeah gonna send files to phil and wen hes had a check ill let u kno

andy

Hi Gary,

Thank you for your email, which I received yesterday. I will send the files to Phil Smith in accounts and, after he has had a look at them, I will be in touch.

Kind regards,

Andrew Scherer

The example above illustrates how different a well-written email and a poorly written one look. It is true that not all work emails need to be as formal as the one above. Over the course of your internship, you will learn which situations allow for a degree of informality (such as short messages to colleagues), and which require you to follow protocol more strictly. If you are ever unsure, ask a colleague to have a quick read over something before you send it (particularly if it is to an external source) and, if in doubt, err on the side of formality. Far better to be too formal than too casual.

Away from linguistic nuances, always ensure you are shown how to use your company's email client at the start of your internship. The majority of firms use Microsoft Outlook, which you may already be familiar with. Even if you feel confident with a program, it is good practice to double-check that you know how to use it properly. It is very important that you have a good grasp of the basics, as you do not want an important email to disappear into the electronic ether never to return, nor do you want to miss a crucial incoming message.

brilliant timesaver

Check whether you have to 'send/receive' manually, or if it is automatic. This is the action that makes your email client retrieve any messages for your account from the server. If it is manual, and you do not click send/receive, then you will not get messages sent to you. If it is automatic, check how often it does a send/receive. Ideally, it should be every 10 to 15 minutes.

One of the great advantages of email is the speed with which you can contact people and information can be distributed. You will therefore be expected to reply to emails promptly. That does not mean you should drop everything you are doing to respond instantly every time you get a message, but you should not leave it two or three days before replying. Just how swiftly you respond depends on the nature of the email and who sent it. If it is a message from a client, you should aim to answer very quickly – within an hour at most. If it is from your manager, you should also look to respond swiftly. A non-urgent message from a colleague should be dealt with within an hour or two.

Internet

Your workstation in the office almost certainly will be connected to the internet and there is a very strong chance you will need to use the web for work purposes. As we discussed in the social media chapter, you may well find certain websites are banned from use. This can range from explicit material to news websites, which are irrelevant for work. It is not a good idea to use the internet for personal purposes at work, as, if you try to access banned websites, it may be recorded and logged against your user name. Only use it for personal reasons if you have been given explicit permission, and it is during your breaks.

You may find, at some point, that a website you need to access for work is being blocked by the company's filter. You will need to talk to your boss, or possibly directly to the IT department, and explain what the website is and why you need it. They should then be able to unblock it.

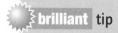 **brilliant** tip

If you are browsing the internet and find a link or something to download that is labelled 'NSFW' then do not click on it. NSFW stands for not safe for work, and the content usually will be explicit or offensive. So don't click!

Phone

Although some companies eschew phone calls in favour of electronic communication, most businesses continue to use phones quite heavily. It is highly likely that you will have to use the phone over the course of your internship and it is therefore wise to enquire whether your company has any guidelines on using it.

Commercial phones normally allow both internal and external calls, so you should make sure you know what you need to do to call a colleague and what you need to press to get an outside line. If you will be using the phone a lot to speak to co-workers it might be worth enquiring if you can have a list of internal numbers. If you are on an external call, you may need to transfer the person to whom you are speaking onto another member of staff, so knowing how to transfer a call to another internal phone is something else you should learn. Also ask whether the phones have a hold or mute function, as it is possible that you will need to put someone on hold when you speak to them (e.g. if you need to check the answer to a question).

Companies may have a set phrase they like their staff to use when answering calls so, if you are not given any guidance on what to say when using the phone, it is worthwhile enquiring if there is anything specific you need to say. As with emails, your level of language should match the person you are speaking to. So, if it is a client, you should be courteous, try to avoid 'fillers' such as um, er, y'know, and do not use slang terms.

Calendars

As part of your internship you may be added to your company's electronic calendar. Although this varies from firm to firm, it usually means that you will be able to see what is in your colleagues' calendars – when they are in the office, when they are at meetings, when they are away – and they in turn can see if you have anything lined up.

If you are added to the company calendar, you should ensure that you write any appointments, meetings or similar in there.

Not only will this help you keep on top of where you have to be and what you have to do, it means your colleagues can see when you are in the office and when not. If your company does not have a general calendar, or if you are not included in it, it is still good practice to keep a record of your schedule for the same reasons. Most computers will have basic calendar software, or it may come as part of your email client (such as in Microsoft Outlook).

Sickness/absence

Inevitably, some people find they need to take some time off during their internship. Sometimes illness or events out of your control will occur and, if they do, you should not feel guilty about needing a few days off. It happens to everyone at some point and, if it is a genuine reason, then your company should be sympathetic to your situation.

Hopefully, during your induction, you will have been given a run-down of what you need to do when taking time off during your internship. This might include information on whom you need to speak to, whether you need to fill in any forms, or any other administrative procedures. If you did not get this information, check with your boss: there may not be any formal steps you need to follow, or your company may have failed to tell you about them.

If you are not going into work because of sickness, and only decide on the day, then you should call your workplace as soon as possible to inform them. Make sure you speak to the right person (this could be directly to your line manager, or to relevant support staff) so that your team knows you will be absent.

brilliant impact

It goes without saying that you should not take time off without a good reason. Having a bit of a cold does not really warrant staying at home, nor does feeling hungover. It is normally acceptable to be absent for very special occasions, such as a graduation day, but I would not suggest asking for a day off so you can go to the sales. The less time you take off, the more committed you will appear.

Remember, an internship is not just a chance for you to learn and develop your skills, it is a great chance to make contacts and build relationships in a chosen industry. If you are constantly taking time off from your internship, you will look uncommitted and uninterested, so do so only if you have to. That said, do not try to haul yourself into work when you are on your last legs and running a 103-degree temperature: that's not commitment, just madness!

Holidays

Depending on the nature of your internship, you may be given a holiday allowance, or you may have a more informal holiday set-up. However, taking holidays is not that advisable if your internship is three months or shorter. Much like taking time off for illness or other reasons, taking holiday during what is a fairly short period of time does not reflect well on your enthusiasm for the internship or the company.

If you already have a holiday when you start your internship, which will require you to take time off, then be up-front about this. Let the company know how much time you need off, and you might want to suggest that, if it is a significant period of time (a week or more), then you would be happy to add the time on to the end of the internship (if this suits your firm). Your company will not be desperately happy if, three weeks into a twelve-week internship, you say you need ten days off because you are going to France with the family.

If your internship is longer than three months, then it is more acceptable to take some time off. Again, I would not advise doing so excessively or trying your best to use up every single bit of holiday allowance, but it is reasonable to have a few days off here and there if you are working for six months.

If your internship is paid, you may be entitled to extra money for any holiday you do not take – so there could be an additional financial incentive not to take any time off!

Office etiquette

If you have not spent much time working in an office before, you may not be particularly *au fait* with everyday office etiquette. This is not something to have major worries about – again your internship is an opportunity for you to learn these sorts of things. However, this section hopefully will outline some of the common nuances you may encounter within a workplace.

If you are making yourself a hot drink – tea, coffee or the like – then it is always good manners to offer to make those around you one as well. If you work in a small office, then maybe offer to make drinks for everyone; if it is a larger office then I would suggest limiting your generosity to those in your immediate vicinity. There is, of course, the perennial image of the 'intern' who, in reality, is just a dogsbody for everyone else at the company, and you should not be expected to make drinks for all your colleagues, all the time. They should repay the favour as well and, if you find you become the only person doing tea rounds, then you should have a word with your boss. However, do not refuse to make people drinks because it is below you – in a well-functioning office everyone from interns to managers should chip in.

Many offices have their own customs for special occasions. For example, if it is someone's birthday they will bring in cake for everyone else to celebrate. Or, at Christmas, the office may run a 'Secret Santa'. Such traditions vary a lot from workplace to workplace, and are not necessarily something you need to ask about. However, it is good to know such things occur, and to keep an eye out for them.

We have already discussed lunch arrangements, and you should get a good idea from your induction of how lunch operates within your office. Nevertheless, you should remember to remain flexible as to when you take lunch, if necessary. Be prepared to put off food for 15 minutes if some work needs finishing and do not be the obstinate person who insists on getting up at 1 pm on the dot every day and not returning a minute before 2 pm. At the same time, be aware that your company should not be making excessive demands on you if you are struggling to fit in a sandwich.

Meetings

Depending on your role and your company, there is a chance you may be asked to accompany colleagues in meetings with people, such as clients or suppliers. As we have discussed, you should make sure you know the dress code for the meeting and if this is different at all from your day-to-day office dress code. If in doubt, make sure you are smarter than normal – you can always take off a tie or a jacket, you can't run home in the middle of a meeting to change out of your trainers.

Before you get to the meeting, ensure you know what your role there is. Your company may be taking you just to allow you to observe and get a feel for meetings. In which case, it would not be appropriate to talk too much, or make observations or suggestions. Obviously, do speak if suitable, but do not try to make yourself an active part of the meeting. If you are going because your company feels you may have something to add or because you have been working on the project the meeting concerns, then do not be too reticent or shy. Offer your opinions and any useful insights you may have. However, do not start complaining about your company, or making suggestions about internal processes – anything like that should be discussed in private, not at an external meeting.

When you get to the meeting, ensure you greet everyone with a smile and a firm handshake, as you would at an interview. Remember, you are not just representing yourself but also your company, and it is very important to give a good first impression. Do your best to try to remember people's names – if you need to ask a question or interject later it will be very helpful.

 **brilliant** recap

- Ensure you produce well-written emails – check them for errors.
- Use the internet for work purposes only.
- Get to know the phone system, including how to put people on hold and transfer calls.
- Use your electronic calendar to keep a record of what you will be doing.
- If you have to take time off, either through sickness or for holiday, inform your manager as early as possible.
- Get to know the norms for your office – from making rounds of hot drinks to lunch arrangements.
- If you go to meetings, make sure you know what your purpose there is (observing or contributing?).

CHAPTER 15

Networking

One great benefit of doing an internship that may continue to be useful for years to come is the networking opportunities it provides. Almost certainly you will meet, and develop relationships with, people who could go on to have a say in your career progression and continuing professional success. Over the course of your internship, you will meet tens, if not hundreds, of new connections, any number of whom could prove to be very valuable further down the line.

There are, of course, ways in which you should go about networking and ways that you should avoid. I would not suggest eyeing up everyone as a potentially useful contact because, apart from anything else, it can be very difficult to second-guess who might be helpful to know later and for what reason. If you do start trying to estimate someone's usefulness, you may start being dismissive of those you feel are irrelevant to you and overly familiar or grovelling to those you believe will be of interest. Rather, you should adopt a level approach to everyone you meet. As ever, firm handshakes, smiles and remembering names all go a long way. If you are offered a business card, take it and thank the person in question – they did not have to give you all their details. If you do not have your own business card (which is very likely), apologise for not being able to reciprocate. You might say you will send them a quick email with your details next time you are at your computer, just in case they are ever needed, or offer to write your email address on one of their own cards.

Having said not to eye up people as potential contacts, clearly you should make a mental note if you meet anyone who is patently of interest, such as a hiring manager. However, the same rules still apply: do not fawn over or flatter people whose help you think you might need, you will just appear disingenuous and shallow. Do email them after meeting them, though, both so they have your details and to help cement yourself in their memory.

brilliant timesaver

If you meet a number of people in a short space of time or in a very busy day, it is easy to forget names or details, so keep your wits about you. It is worth having a dedicated place on your desk or at home to keep business cards you receive to ensure you don't lose them – you will kick yourself if you have met someone useful then cannot find their details when you need them.

This chapter will specifically have a look at four different groups of people who potentially could be useful to you in the future, and how to deal with them accordingly.

Colleagues

Naturally, your colleagues will make up a good proportion of the new people you meet during your internship. Working alongside them every day should give you a good chance to get to know them and is a great way to network.

Often it is very useful to ask how workmates have got to where they are today. People are normally more than happy to talk about themselves and their achievements, so you should be able to gain some good insights into what paths they have followed. This may give you some fresh ideas on entry routes into professions you had not previously thought about. They might also be able to offer some of their own tips and hints that they picked up along the way. This could be anything from which professional bodies you should contact, to which companies are open to speculative applications. They might even have their own contacts that they are willing to share with you.

When talking with colleagues about these sorts of things it is usually better to do so in more casual surroundings and not take a formal approach. An email with a list of questions is far less likely to elicit a positive response than just having a chat over lunch where you can demonstrate your interest and enthusiasm far more effectively. Most people are prepared to help others just starting out in their industry with bits of advice and guidance. Just how helpful people are will vary from person to person. Some younger colleagues may be more forthcoming with assistance as their own move from education to work will still be fresh in their minds; some may see you as competition so may hold back slightly. Similarly, older workmates may help out as they are not threatened by you; though some may have forgotten how difficult it is to start your career and may feel you should receive only limited favours. Remember: never be afraid to ask for help – the worst that will happen is that someone will say no.

When you finish your internship, ensure that you have the details of those colleagues whom you would feel comfortable contacting in the future to ask for more advice or help and, if there are any you got on well with, then stay in touch. You don't need to give them your ongoing life story, but a quick email every now and again to see how they are and let them know how you are doing is suitable. Part 3 of the book will look at staying in touch with your host company in much greater detail.

Boss and mentor

While it is generally best to network with colleagues and ask them career-related questions in a more casual manner, you should approach networking with your boss and mentor with a greater level of formality. You will probably have fewer chances to talk to them in informal settings so this is partly necessity but, more importantly, they have a certain duty to help you with networking and give advice on your future professional path. You should therefore feel happy asking questions of your boss or mentor when you have meetings to discuss how your internship is progressing.

In terms of your future at the company where you are interning, you should have had a good idea of what chances there were for you to become a permanent employee there when you started the placement. It is not suitable to keep asking about how likely it is you will be taken on permanently, either at the end of your internship or further down the line, but you should be able to get an idea of your chances from general feedback.

It is less appropriate to ask your boss or mentor directly how they got to where they are today, as you would a colleague: it may appear impertinent. That is not to say, however, that you should avoid talking about their background or progression, just do so with a little more subtlety. Ask if they have any specific advice for someone trying to break into the industry and perhaps whether they have any 'insider' hints. That should encourage them to offer up some information on their own past and what they feel you need to do to progress.

Do not limit networking with your superiors to your own boss. Do a bit of research; find out if any other managers within your company might be useful to talk to. You may be interested in other sectors in which your firm operates, or a different department from your own. It could then be very beneficial talking to other people higher up both to seek advice and to create contacts for the future – and what better time to do it than when you are also working at the same business.

If you are approaching people who work for the same company, but with whom you have not come into direct contact, then try to get someone who knows both you and them to make an introduction. This can be in person or via email. Alternatively, see if you have something in common – you may have gone to the same university, you may live close by, you may even support the same football team. You can then use this as a way to introduce yourself.

When first getting in touch you should be very polite and apologise for disturbing them, then state who you are and ask if they have just a couple of minutes of spare time to offer you some advice or have a quick chat. Hopefully, they will be receptive and either give you some help by email or, if you're lucky, set up an informal meeting. You can then approach talking to them as you would with your own boss.

As with colleagues, it is a good idea to stay in contact with any relevant superiors, as we shall see in Part 3.

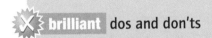 **brilliant** dos and don'ts

Networking with managers

Do

✔ Maintain a respectable level of formality

✔ Try to network with other senior members of staff in the company

Don't

✘ Pester bosses or mentors about future employment opportunities

✘ Ask too many questions about their own employment background

Fellow interns

Over the course of your internship there is a good chance you will meet other interns, either within your own department, elsewhere within your company, or working for other firms. You may at first think it irrelevant to network with other people at the same stage as you, still looking for their first job. However, having such contacts can prove very advantageous both during your job-hunt and in the future.

Fellow interns will have developed their own valuable experience within their placement, some of which may differ from your own experience. This could range from practical knowledge of working methods to important insights into their company.

If the interns you meet are working at the same company as you they may have learned things that you have not yet, or vice versa. By way of example, they may know a certain colleague places great emphasis on presentation, or that one manager is particularly receptive to interns asking for advice. Such knowledge can be hugely useful during your placement, helping boost your own performance.

If the interns work for another company, they may be able to offer both a view of their firm and an external take on the company at which you are interning. Naturally, these may be biased, but nevertheless interesting to hear.

Given fellow interns are in the same position as you, seeking permanent employment, they are likely to have their ear to the ground in terms of potential jobs. It can be very useful to share any information.

brilliant tip

Be open with fellow interns. Exchange ideas, sources and bits of information. Developing this openness and camaraderie could yield benefits in both the short and long term. Do not, however, compromise your own position by telling people absolutely everything about your job applications. Exercise some caution.

It is likely that some of the interns you come across will be cagey and unforthcoming with any information or help. This is only natural: some people will see you purely as competition. Do not take it personally, but long term it is far better to have a reputation as someone who is helpful and open rather than closed and distrusting. That is not to say you should sing it from the rooftops if you have a potential job offer lined up – that may encourage other applications, which could derail your own – but be open with general information and tips. You never know when a good favour will be repaid. For example, if you develop good relationships with fellow interns and they find a job before you, they may be able to put in a good word for you with their new employer.

Clients

Networking with clients is a very different proposition to developing contacts within your own company or among fellow interns. First and foremost you have to always bear in mind you are representing your company, not yourself, when talking to clients. Your firm probably will not take kindly to you trying to talk to clients for personal reasons when you are meant to be conducting business for them, or that you are bothering the business's customers.

Far better is to allow a relationship with any clients you work with to develop naturally within the context of your internship tasks. Do not ask any questions or favours for personal purposes during your placement. Rather, at the end of your internship, ask any clients with whom you have struck up a rapport whether they might mind you getting in touch in the future for a bit of advice on the basis you will be leaving your current employers shortly. Ensure that you have any relevant contact details safely noted down before you leave your placement.

If any clients are happy to offer you some help in the future then, like colleagues or even bosses, they may offer advice, industry insight, or even let you know if their company is hiring at all.

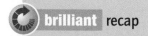 recap

- Be aware that everyone you meet is a potentially useful contact.

- Use informal chats with colleagues to get career tips and advice.

- If you have the opportunity, talk to more senior staff to see if they can offer any help.

- Do not ignore your peers. Fellow interns may also have useful insights to offer.

- If you have developed a good working relationship with any clients, then try approaching them for help after your internship.

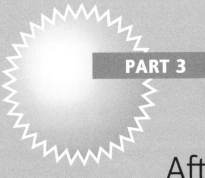

PART 3

After your internship

Your internship is coming to an end. Hopefully, you have learned a lot and had an enjoyable time. Perhaps you are preparing to pack up your desk, say your goodbyes and bid a tearful farewell to the office. There is, however, still plenty of work you can do to ensure your internship continues to be of great use to you. This section is all about helping you utilise your internship as much as possible after it has finished, from getting a permanent job to presenting your new experience as well as possible on your CV.

CHAPTER 16

Securing that job

As we all know, internships are ultimately a step on the road to employment. Therefore, one of the most crucial aspects of your internship – securing a permanent employment – comes after it is over. Whether you have decided your internship has helped you find your calling or if you want a complete change of scene, this chapter aims to walk you through post-internship job-hunting.

Deciding whether you want to stay

The first question you need to ask yourself is whether you want to stay at your internship host company. If you are a graduate, this probably will mean moving straight from your internship into a permanent position. If you are still in education, it is more likely to be a contract starting at an agreed date after the completion of your studies. Either way, you should give some serious thought to whether staying at the company is the right move for you. Taking a decision on a job has consequences different from choosing an internship and these need careful consideration.

Naturally, one of the first things you will consider is whether you have found your internship to be a positive experience. Be realistic when looking back over your time at the company and try to take an overall view. Do not let a few bad days or frustrating moments cloud your judgement: absolutely everyone has to deal with times like that at work. Instead you should consider more generally: have I found the work stimulating? Does my boss appreciate my work? Do I get on with my colleagues? Would I like to continue doing this sort of thing in the short to medium term? If you answer yes to most or all of these, then you may well be onto a winner. However, deciding to stay is not just a question of whether you had a good time during your internship, though that should factor into your decision. There are also more far-reaching implications of turning an internship into a job that you need to bear in mind.

brilliant tip

Before accepting or declining any permanent position at your internship company, ask yourself these questions:

● Did I get on with my colleagues?

● Did I find the work stimulating?

● Will the work change if I become a permanent employee?

● Will my hours change?

● What are my job prospects in the medium to long term?

● What direction is the company taking in the short to medium term?

The big question, from a practical point of view, is how much the job will differ from your internship on a day-to-day basis. During your internship you may well have worked basic office hours of 9–5, or similar. If you become a full-time member of staff, will you be required to stay longer? Do not just assume that you will be free to go at 5 pm on the dot every day – if you are a paid employee, then sometimes you may be expected to finish work beyond 'normal' leaving time.

You also need to find out what extra responsibilities you will or will not receive on turning your internship permanent. Probably you will be keen to take on some extra work and demonstrate you are a worthy new member of the full-time team, but you do not want to have too much loaded on you. You do not want to compromise either your ability to get things done or your enjoyment of your job, so make sure there is a balance between new challenges and a realistic workload.

Similarly, you should establish what path for progression exists and what kind of timeline is typical for moving up the company ladder. In some firms they will expect you to undertake your entry-level role for two years or more before considering you for promotion. In other companies they may be happy to move you up after six months, if you have proved yourself capable. Ensure that the culture of promotion of the business in question matches your ambitions. If you are looking for quick advancement, then staying somewhere that offers little chance for promotion in the short term will not be right for you. Similarly, if you want to cement your knowledge of a role before looking to move up the chain, then a company that wants someone to progress to management swiftly might not be a good match.

Another factor to consider is the long-term plans of the company itself. If you have been working within a small company and particularly liked its size, then you should establish what its expansion plans are. If it has just received investment or is growing rapidly, you may find that six months down the line there are 50 per cent more staff and the atmosphere has changed. Ask yourself whether you would still be happy at the company if this is the case. Such growth may also affect your own promotion prospects – either positively (as a longer-serving member of the team you are more likely to have new staff working under you) or negatively (there is more competition).

It is also valuable to compare your own internship experiences with those of your friends. An internship may be your first experience of the professional world, so comparing and contrasting with others in your position will help you gain some perspective on how it really went. You may find your opinions change – for good or for bad – when you hear what your peers got up to on their internships.

brilliant tip

It never hurts to have a look around the job market and see what alternatives to staying at your internship company exist. You may find that there are plenty of firms hiring in your sector, and you may know from hearsay that lots of people are having success in securing jobs. If so, you can afford to be a little more choosy when deciding to stay at your internship. Conversely, you may know plenty of people struggling to find work, so exercising some prudence may be called for. While I wouldn't advise abandoning your dreams of an ideal job, sometimes you need to be willing to compromise. This is particularly true in the early stages of your career in what is currently a tough job market.

Meeting your boss/mentor

Of course, all of the above is purely academic if there is no position to be had after your internship, or if your company decides you are not suited enough to stay on after your internship. It is therefore wise to ensure you have a meeting with your boss, your mentor, or both towards the scheduled end of your placement to talk about your fledgling career.

There is a fine line to tread between being pushy about receiving the offer of a permanent job and legitimately establishing what chance you have of staying on. Some companies may schedule a formal discussion in the last week or two of your internship with the purpose of talking about your performance and whether your future lies there or elsewhere. This is particularly likely to happen if they have expressly said there is the opportunity to earn full-time employment after the placement. If this is the case you need not pester your superiors about your future – they will already be considering it carefully. If you need an answer sooner than any scheduled meeting, for example if you have another potential job offer, then ask if it is possible to have the talk brought forward and explain your reasons why. If there is a legitimate basis to do so, particularly one that is time-pressured, your company should be happy to oblige. After all, it is in their interests to sort out your future too.

If there has been no meeting scheduled, and you are unsure where you stand with regards to ongoing employment, then you have every right to ask to talk about it with a manager or mentor. That is not to say you should walk into their office and demand a meeting, rather towards the end of your internship ask if they can spare some time to talk about how you have done and your future.

If your superiors feel you have not done enough to warrant a full-time job, you are entitled to ask why. You should then receive feedback relating to your performance and, in particular, to areas in which you did not do so well. You might find it useful to ask for written feedback rather than just hearing it in person, as this will give you a chance to read it over more than once and see if you feel it is a fair reflection. It will also prove useful to have a written record to refer back to. If you believe the assessment of your work is unfair, then raise your concerns with your manager or mentor. You should, however, always remain calm and level-headed when discussing such things, even if you feel strongly about it. Raising your voice or displaying any anger will not help your cause.

If the company makes it clear that, in principle, they would like to take you on but there is no position available within the company, and of course you wish to stay, make sure that they know to contact you should any roles open up. In the meantime, ask if they can offer any assistance with your job-hunt elsewhere, put in a good word for you or recommend avenues to pursue. If you have done a good job, they should be more than willing to help.

Speaking to colleagues

It can be a good idea to talk to your colleagues to get an idea of how you are doing, and to see if they have any insight into opportunities for permanent employment. Often, this is done best in a casual setting, at lunch or after work, for example. Naturally, most people will not say to your face if they think you have done badly, but you should be able to get an idea from the strength of their reactions roughly how well they think you have been performing. Do not feel like you have to leave this right until the end of your internship – it can be very useful to hear these kinds of informal comments on your work all the way through the placement. Your colleagues also might be able to give you the inside track on how many interns have gone on to earn full-time positions; they may have even been interns themselves originally.

brilliant impact

If you have made an effort to get to know your colleagues during your internship, it will be far easier to approach them for advice about future work and they will be far more likely to offer positive words on your behalf if they are asked about your long-term suitability for a job.

Moving on

If, after careful consideration, you have decided you do not want to stay with the company beyond your internship or you have not been offered a position, then you need to put your additional experience to good use when finding a new job. The following chapters will look in greater detail at references and how to optimise your CV. However, there are several additional things worth noting.

If you are considering changing the sector in which you want to work, you can still use your internship to help inform your future choices and boost any applications. Think about the aspects of your internship that you particularly enjoyed and the tasks that you did not like so much. Think about sectors and jobs in which you will be doing more of the former and less of the latter.

brilliant example

Having done a journalism internship, you decide that your instinct for a news story is lacking and you dislike pitching ideas to editors. However, you did relish the writing side of the job. Why not consider being a copywriter? Instead of finding your own stories, you will be writing to a brief and, increasingly, working with digital elements like search engine optimisation and tracking tools.

You should also remember that applying for jobs can almost be a full-time job in itself. So do not expect to get plenty of applications out while you are still interning. Make sure you apply for the most relevant positions available and spend time tailoring your CV and cover letter. Far better to send two well thought-out applications than half a dozen ones that seem to show a lack of effort.

 **brilliant** recap

● Before deciding whether you want to stay, have a long think about how you feel the internship went, from relationships with colleagues to the tasks you completed.

● Ensure you have a meeting with your boss and/or mentor before the end of your placement to discuss how you have done and any potential future work.

● Talk to colleagues to see if they think you would fit in as a permanent employee and to get their views on the company as an employer.

● Remember that your internship experience is still useful, even if you want to change sector.

CHAPTER 17

Your reference

Getting a good reference can be a very valuable part of your internship. References are vital for securing future work – rarely will you get a new job without one. Employers also place greater emphasis on professional references over academic or personal ones, so having one from a company where you have spent several months will add weight to any future job applications.

Preparations for your reference

It is worth asking at the start of your internship, or even before it begins, whether your employer will be able to provide a reference for you after the placement if your work is of a suitable standard. Do not demand one, particularly if you are yet to spend any actual time in the office, but it is always good to remind your company that a reference is important to you. The host company should be more than happy to oblige.

To secure a good reference, it is important to work hard and behave professionally throughout your internship. Naturally, any business is far more likely to provide you with a strong recommendation if they feel you have proved yourself to be a good member of staff than if you contribute little during your placement. If you do display a lack of interest or motivation when interning, then the company may still give you some kind of reference, but it may not be in the most glowing terms.

However, you should not fret about your reference if you make some mistakes over the course of your internship. It is completely normal that, as an intern who is learning all the time, you will not do everything perfectly and mistakes do happen. Employers will not go into details and specifics in a reference, and will take into account the fact you are with them to learn, not to complete tasks perfectly every time. Far more important is the general picture your host company builds of you: your attitude, your commitment, your ability to develop and improve. If you work hard, you should expect a positive reference.

brilliant tip

If you are concerned that, for whatever reason, your company may not give you a very positive reference, then it is best to raise this when you ask for one rather than leave it and potentially jeopardise any future job applications. You should avoid being confrontational about it – this will exacerbate any underlying issues and do more harm than good. Admit that you have been disappointed with how you have performed in the area of concern and express your worries that it might blight your reference. Your employer should, hopefully, talk you through their own thoughts and reassure you if they are not planning to let it affect your reference.

Putting a referee on your CV

If your company is happy to provide you with a reference, that does not necessarily mean they will write one straight away. It is far more common for businesses to allow you to put them down on your CV as a potential reference; they will then provide one when requested by any future employer of yours.

The next chapter will examine in more depth how to present your new CV, but we will have a quick look at displaying references here. There are normally two ways in which references appear on a CV. The first is simply a line at the end of the final page, stating 'References are available on request'. This is sufficient to let the potential employer know that you have at least one person willing to corroborate the information you have given and to speak positively on your behalf. However, it does not let the company know who exactly the referee is.

Once you have done an internship, you should have a new referee that, if you are planning to apply for positions in a similar industry, will be particularly relevant to your applications. It can therefore be better to name them up front. This will make your application stronger: the person reading it knows you have sufficiently impressed someone with a connection to the industry or role to vouch for your ability.

Normally you will be expected to provide two references when applying for jobs. Before doing an internship, this might have been an academic reference (from your tutor) and a professional reference from someone who managed you before – perhaps from a summer job. With your new reference you will have to drop one of these two. Normally it is better to retain the academic reference while you are still a recent graduate – your tutor should know you well enough to offer informed opinions to employers, as well as backing up your academic record. You can then replace the older, less relevant professional referee with the one gained from your internship experience.

brilliant example

When applying for your internship you had two referees – your tutor from university, and your manager from your part-time job at the local supermarket. You let employers know you were happy to give them by putting 'References available on request' at the end of your CV.

After your three-month internship at a small digital marketing company, you can now include the head of the firm among your referees. So now, when applying for a job, instead of stating 'References available on request' at the bottom of your CV, you list your new referee's full name, job title and contact details. Next to this is your academic reference. Companies reading your application know you have a relevant, and influential, person willing to testify to your work and character.

Finally, always remember to double-check that the people you list on your CV are still happy to provide a reference each time you send a new application. There should not be any reason why they would say no, but it is polite and good practice to warn them when you are passing on their details and inviting another firm to contact them.

Written reference

An alternative (or an addition) to giving a referee's details on your CV is to secure a written reference from them at the end of your internship. Normally this will outline the tasks you completed during your internship, your strengths as a potential employee, and any additional information your referee feels would be relevant for future job applications.

Often this will come in letter form (addressed 'To whom it may concern'). Whoever has written it will then sign the letter, and should either print it on headed paper or stamp it with a company logo to reassure anyone reading it that it is genuine.

Getting this kind of letter of recommendation is very useful for three reasons. Firstly, it could mean that a new employer does not have to take the time to call or write to your referee. Producing a letter that has already been written could save them hassle and makes you look efficient. Secondly, it suggests you impressed your previous company enough during your internship that they felt they should write a specific letter to talk about your positives and not just be listed as a potential reference.

Finally, a letter of recommendation should be a very quotable source for any applications you make. It is one thing saying you are hardworking and proficient with photo-editing software, for example, but it is far better to quote an employer praising your work ethic and ability with Photoshop.

It is also a good idea to check that they would be happy still to be listed as a referee in case any future employers wish to double-check anything in the letter or find out more about you. You do not want to be in a situation where your internship company has provided you with a written reference but has not made itself available to confirm its veracity!

brilliant tip

Use a letter of recommendation like a film poster uses positive reviews. Pick out short, sharp sentences or phrases that demonstrate your ability and use them in an application. This could be part of an answer on an application form or it could be in your personal statement on your CV: 'I have a strong desire to work in the graphic design industry, with my internship in the sector having helped me develop "a strong eye for striking design with real impact" (Sarah Smith, CEO Bells Design Agency).'

Not the be-all and end-all

Of course, you should never lose sight of the fact that a reference is only one part of a job application. It is by no means the be-all and end-all when trying to secure a new position. As I have already suggested, do not panic if you felt you made a few mistakes during your internship, which might have a negative impact on your reference. Companies will take a broad view of your placement, and not judge you on one or two errors. This is even truer if the reference is required several months after you finish – employers will rely on overall impression far more than details that they may already have forgotten.

If you are concerned that your reference may contain the odd negative point, it is also worth remembering that often all referees need to do is confirm you were at the company when you said you were. Frequently this can be enough to satisfy the HR department at your new company, which has to tick boxes rather than build an in-depth look at your past.

Finally, always bear in mind that, for the majority of businesses, a reference will not be the thing that gets you a job. The things that matter are your CV, cover letter, application and interview – you will be the person who earns the job, not a reference. The only time a reference will have a major impact on gaining work is if it does not match what you have said you have done or match the skills you have said you have. If this does happen (it is extremely rare, unless you actually lie on your CV), you still may be able to explain any differences that your new employer feels exist between what you and your referee have said.

 brilliant recap

- Confirm at the start of your internship that your company will be happy to provide a reference, if your work is of a suitable standard.

- Commitment and hard work will yield a positive reference, even if you make some mistakes along the way.

- Check with your referee every time you give out their details.

- A letter of recommendation is impressive for potential employers and can save them time.

- Remember: references are not the be-all and end-all in job applications.

CHAPTER 18

Your new CV

aving completed an internship, you now have a major new addition to your CV: you can demonstrate a whole new set of skills and experience to potential employers in addition to your academic and extra-curricular activities. You may well find yourself with the enviable headache of having a bit too much to squeeze onto your CV and needing to cut it down. This is really positive – you can make your applications even more focused and tailored to each job by picking and choosing the aspects of your background that are most relevant. This chapter will help you put this new experience into your CV in the best way possible.

Education or experience?

Earlier in this book we talked about preparing your CV for internship applications and advised you to put your education ahead of employment history, as it generally interests employers more. With a few months of relevant professional experience under your belt, you may be reconsidering this arrangement and want to place your internship higher up on your CV.

Having the extra work experience certainly does make it a more difficult decision when choosing what to prioritise in job applications. There is no hard and fast rule for what to focus on in your CV after doing an internship; it comes down to a personal judgement call as to what you feel an employer will value most highly.

On balance, the answer is probably that it is still best to start your CV with your degree and education. Ultimately, you have spent much more time working towards it and it gives a good indication of your overall competence. However, this will not hold true for every single person. If your internship is extremely relevant to a position that you have applied for, or was a longer placement, then you might consider highlighting it first. You could then mention in your cover letter, or the personal statement on your CV, that you have a degree to avoid confusion over your qualifications. You might also consider putting your internship experience ahead of your degree, if you feel the latter is irrelevant or not strong enough to grab an employer's attention.

As with your pre-internship CV, it is worth listing relevant modules from your education. These still offer hiring managers a good insight into your knowledge, and can complement your professional experience nicely. Of course, it is important to be strict when choosing what to include and what to miss off – with your extra experience, you do not want to waste space or distract someone reading your CV with material that is not pertinent.

brilliant tip

Do not dismiss your degree as something to relegate to the bottom of your CV now you have done an internship. Remember: it took you three or more years to earn your degree and it shows plenty of very useful skills. If your internship is extremely pertinent to a job application, you may consider putting it ahead of your education, but do not take this decision lightly. Your degree is still one of your biggest facets.

What to include

Over the course of your internship you were, undoubtedly, exposed to lots of new work practices and learned a huge amount. The key to creating a successful new CV with all your additional knowledge is to pick out the most relevant aspects and present them in an attractive and informative manner.

One of the most effective CV tools that your internship can equip you with is real-life examples – including facts and figures – of how you have applied yourself in the workplace. This is where keeping a diary or a portfolio of your work will come in very useful. Having all the tasks you completed and relevant statistics to hand will make writing your new CV a lot easier and will help you target it more effectively. Hard evidence to back up assertions is a key part of a successful CV: use what you did during your internship to prove how valuable you can be as an employee.

 **example**

Which of the following bullet points on a CV do you think will impress an employer more?

- I contributed to the company's blog, often writing a post every week.

- I regularly wrote for the company blog. During this period, traffic to the website increased by 12 per cent and average dwell time increased to 6.43 minutes.

When writing about your internship on your CV, it is a very wise idea to say if you worked with any clients during the placement. This will show that you have commercial experience beyond just one office and also that your company placed sufficient trust in you to allow you to work directly with their customers. It can be particularly impressive if you can drop in a big company name, although a small one can be just as effective, if you explain what they do and how you worked with them. It is even worth mentioning if you spent time observing a team working for a client but were not actively involved yourself – at the very least the person reading your application knows you have been exposed to client-facing work.

If you have learned how to use any specialist software during your internship, be sure to include this in your new CV, too. For example, if you did an accountancy placement and had training in Sage software, then this is a big facet that employers love to see. It is always a good idea to include software competency, even if you think it is entirely irrelevant to the position to which you are applying. You never know when an employer may need someone with that particular knowledge and it demonstrates your ability to pick up new computer skills quickly.

What to leave off

Now you have lots more experience to put on your CV you will, inevitably, have to cut out some of the things that featured on it before you had done an internship. This can be a tricky task and, as we've seen, will differ for each job for which you apply.

There may be some things that were previously included in your CV, which obviously no longer hold any relevance to future jobs. Before you completed an internship, you may have mentioned summer jobs you did while still at school. It is these kinds of entries that can be deleted from your CV to make way for your new professional experience. Similarly, some of the extra-curricular activities from school or university that you previously listed may no longer be worthy of a place (although do not get rid of all your extra-curricular stuff – employers like to see you are a normal human being with interests!).

It may be tougher to choose between more recent additions to your CV when deciding what to filter out and what should remain. Is your year as treasurer of the netball club more important than the two weeks' work experience you did at a law firm?

Will your stint as director of a musical for the university theatre club impress a hiring manager more than a summer working in a children's summer camp? The answer, frustrating as it may be, is that it will vary from job application to job application. For every application, you need to ask yourself exactly what the employer is looking for and identify where your background matches these requirements. Writing out a list of what qualities you feel the successful candidate will possess can be a useful aid.

brilliant tip

Every time you are adapting your CV for a new application, make a list, in order of importance, of 10 things the employer wants to see in a candidate. You should then check this against your CV to ensure you are demonstrating competency in as many requirements as possible, with greatest focus on the top two or three. If you are struggling to match the skills and background that are called for, then you need to have another look at what has made it onto your CV, or even reconsider whether you are suitable for the role.

As mentioned earlier, it is always a good idea to include any specialist software that you feel comfortable using, even if it is not obviously relevant for your new job. You should not, however, list every single piece of software that you can use. It will be taken as a given that you can use Microsoft Word and use emails, so do not list these individually. If you are happy using the basic functions of Word, PowerPoint, Excel, etc. then you can simply list 'Microsoft Office' as one of your abilities. Of course, if the job requires a deeper understanding of Excel or lesser used programs such as Access, then do make it clear that you have experience of them.

 **brilliant** recap

- Normally, education will still come above your internship experience on your CV.

- Use facts and figures to demonstrate your experience effectively.

- Remove older and more irrelevant aspects from your CV – old summer jobs, for example.

- Ultimately, putting together your new CV is a balancing act and will require some judgement calls.

CHAPTER 19

Staying in touch

Staying in touch with the company where you interned is always a good idea, regardless of whether you are interested in future employment there or not. Of course, if you have already secured a job where you interned, then you probably won't need this chapter. If you are leaving the company after your internship, then the following pages should give you some good tips for how to stay in touch.

One of your main motivations for staying in touch may be the potential for future work. This does not necessarily have to be limited to a permanent, full-time position. Students who intern in their summer holidays sometimes receive freelance work from their company while they are still studying – a very nice way to supplement your student loan. However, even if getting more work with the firm is not something that interests you (perhaps having secured a job elsewhere), then it is still very valuable to maintain contact with your former workplace. You never know when you may need the help or advice of your old colleagues, or when knowing someone in that industry will prove to be useful to your new job. It is always wise to maintain strong links within your professional network, and staying in touch with the company where you interned is a good way to start this.

Official record

The first thing to do when looking to maintain contact with your company, particularly if it is with a view to employment at a later date, is to ask to be kept on record as having been an intern there. If it is a larger company, then this is something to talk about with the HR department. They will have records of former employees and can make a note on your file that you would like to be considered for vacant positions when they arise. It also means that, should you ever need to call up again, they will have all the details of your internship available.

brilliant tip

Larger companies sometimes run alumni networks for their former employees. It could be worth checking whether you qualify to join, as it will help you maintain a good link with the business and can be fantastic for networking. Also, if there is a newsletter or similar for former employees, then make sure you sign up to receive it. Again, this will keep you in the loop regarding company news and it may advertise internal vacancies.

If you have worked for a smaller company, there is a good chance it will not have so many official processes for former employees. It is therefore important that you make it clear to your manager and colleagues if you would be interested in permanent work further down the line, should it become available. You should also be more proactive in following other suggestions for staying in touch if more formal methods are limited.

Email

Using email is a very quick and easy way to stay in touch with former colleagues or managers from your internship. Sending an occasional email to someone you worked with during your internship will keep you at the forefront of their minds and should engender a greater willingness from them to help you, should you ever require it. You are far less likely to get a positive response to a request for help or advice if you send an email out of the blue 12 months after your internship, having been silent up until that point. Always ensure that you reply swiftly if your former company emails you – preferably on the same day. Leave it much longer and you can appear rude and uninterested (unless of course you have a genuine reason for doing so, such as being on holiday).

There is, of course, a careful line to tread between being friendly and spamming people. If you start emailing people you worked with once a week, or even once every few weeks, then they will start ignoring your messages very quickly. Similarly, if you start sending a message on the first Monday of every month simply for the sake of it, asking the same questions and offering little relevant conversation, then you will also be doing more harm than good. Make sure you email every now and again but, more importantly, make sure you are sending an email that someone will want to read. Things such as a comment on a relevant news story or an offer of help will be welcome. A list of perfunctory questions and a quick update on how your university football team are getting on will not be. If you have former colleagues who you genuinely consider to be friends, then of course go ahead and stay in touch as you would normally – you don't need an excuse to have a chat with your mates.

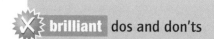 **brilliant** dos and don'ts

When staying in touch with former colleagues by email

Do

✔ Try to get in touch once every three or four months

✔ Make sure you are saying something relevant in the email (e.g. offer congratulations if the firm has won an award)

✔ Reply very promptly if you receive an email. Leaving it much longer than a day can be considered rude

Don't

✘ Send messages with monotonous regularity. If you email every fortnight, you become a spammer

✘ Fill the email with platitudes, mindless questions and irrelevant news (e.g. 'How are you? How is work? I'm pretty well, got a big essay at the moment!')

Online

Another great way of keeping up with a company is online. Checking the firm's website every now and again will ensure you are on top of major news. Even more useful is social media. Although not every business has a social media presence, large numbers have already started harnessing Twitter, Facebook and the like for commercial purposes. Such platforms should give you a more in-depth insight into what is happening at your company and keep you abreast of any developments within the organisation. Make sure you like, follow or are connected with both the company and relevant employees (such as your erstwhile manager), if they also have a presence. Your social media feed will then do the job of keeping you up to date with useful information.

The beauty of social media is that you can do more than just passively follow developments online. You can continue to really engage with the company by offering your thoughts on a posting or helping to disseminate the information they share. Comment on LinkedIn discussions, respond to Facebook posts, reply to tweets and interact with blogs: all of these actions will help remind the company of your interest in them, and help show how engaged with relevant topics you are. A word of caution, however: like email, do try to avoid doing this in a spammy way. Liking every single thing a company puts on Facebook probably will be seen as a bit odd, rather than very keen, so stick to the usual rules of engagement. Also, remember that, if your comments are only ever along the lines of 'Great!' or 'Really good post!', then you are not demonstrating engagement but the exact opposite. So, once again, ensure that your communication is meaningful.

Socialising

Just because you have left a company does not mean you have to cut off all social ties with it. Often firms will invite former interns to any social events they are holding, particularly ones with whom they have stayed in contact. Do your best to go to any events to which you are invited, as you did when you were still interning. While emails and social media can be great for regular contact, particularly from a distance, nothing beats seeing someone in person for keeping up good relations.

This does not necessarily have to be a major party – sometimes it can be better to pop along to after-work drinks on a Friday. Or, if you do not live close to the company, let them know if you are ever in the area and ask if it would be OK to pop by and say hello. Essentially, you need to ensure that, after finishing your internship, you do not disappear off the face of the planet or become someone who exists only online.

 **brilliant** recap

- If the company holds records of former employees, ask to be included, and state that you would be interested in future work.

- Use email to stay in touch with former colleagues, but be careful not to inundate them with messages.

- Follow the company's website and social media presence to stay up to date with their news.

- Continue to get involved with company socials, if you are invited.

Conclusion

As I hope you have discovered from reading this book, there is a lot more to an internship than the pejorative cliché of getting the coffee and doing the photocopying. Internships have become a crucial stepping stone in the path from education to work. They will provide you with additional skills, experience and contacts as well as helping you decide what career path is right for you. Graduates trying to secure a first job after finishing university will increasingly find themselves at a major disadvantage if they have not completed at least one period of serious work experience. Where this might once have been two weeks of work shadowing, employers now expect their new hires to demonstrate that they can apply their knowledge in a professional context. An internship gives you the opportunity to do just that.

It would be remiss to ignore the fact that internships have been the subject of some negative attention in the press, with tales of unscrupulous companies taking advantage of desperate graduates and using them as free labour. It is important to remember that these are not real internships, merely unprincipled businesses using the internship mantle to disguise poor employment practice. Do not let such horror stories put you off doing an internship. As we have seen throughout the book it could be one of the most important parts of your fledgling career. Just bear in mind the advice from Chapter 5 on avoiding bad internships and you should find your placement is both hugely beneficial and enjoyable.

It is never too early to start thinking about doing an internship. Don't put it off until after you graduate. Why not look into doing a part-time placement alongside your studies? Companies are increasingly offering students the chance to go into their office one or two days a week to gain extra experience while they complete their degrees. Alternatively use the long vacations that you are afforded by university education to get that extra experience. Steal the march on your peers who start thinking about life after university only when they have a mortar board on their head and a degree in their hand.

If you have reached graduation without having done an internship then fear not. There are still lots of opportunities to do a placement after leaving university and it is important to remain upbeat and proactive as you try to get onto the first rung of the career ladder. If you take on board some of the advice and tips contained in this book you should be on the right track to land a meaningful and beneficial placement.

It is always worth remembering that an internship is ultimately a means to an end. No one wants to be an intern all their life. Internships are fantastic for helping you decide which job is right for you, gaining extra experience and making your first contacts in the business world. All of these things, however, are simply additional facets in your pursuit of gainful employment. If your placement doesn't live up to your expectations, if you don't get on that well with your colleagues, if it turns out that your dream career isn't actually all you thought it would be, then your internship is still very valuable: far better to go through the trial and error process of finding the best position for your skills in a temporary set-up which you can easily leave than a month into a permanent job.

I hope this book has been a useful accompaniment to your internship experience and has helped you forge a path through the occasionally daunting world of internships. I wish you the very best of luck with your first steps into the world of work.